Soulward

POEMS AND PROSE

J. Wilder

Soulward
Poems and Prose

Cover art by Sarah Hansen of Okay Creations.

Soulward

Chorus Ghost

the radio pauses
between songs
leaving a lurching silence
then comes a simple melody
circling and soothing and sensual
and between the lines and the lyrics
looms a beast
raising its head
baleful glittering eyes fixed on me
through the sentences and notes like prison bars
the beast is memory
wrapping and winding about me in a python grip
coils of context and vision
remembrance of curtains of long dark hair
hiding farewell tears
there are packed and stuffed between stanzas
years of turmoil and anguish
leavened by golden afternoons cruising
high on each other
silence resting between us
comfortable and companionable
a space filled by smooth notes sang low
exhortations to hike up your skirt a little more
she does
then comes the chorus crashing into me

a flash flood assaults me
debris and detritus of past lives
building around me
drowning me
the song begins to fade
the sharp constricting claws
of the memory beast
which is song
uncurl reluctantly
leaving me gasping
hearing ghosts of that haunted refrain
(come and crash into me)
lingering with visceral force
like the dancing shadows
from staring too long at the sun
the radio pauses between songs
leaving a lurching silence
and only bruises remain

Silence Broken

temper temper little Athena
my volatile Persephone
so warlike in all your rage
whose force flattens trees
flinging shrapnel like hurled daggers
into my solitude
into our fragile peace
creating anger-explosions like hurricanes
temper temper little Athena
sheathe your hungry swords
rest your raging stabbing spears
come away with me
explore the gentle night with me
be my Venus
not Vesuvius
express exultations
not explosions
temper temper little Athena
douse your shouts to whispers
this endless anger reverberates
tolls like bells of war
your voice was meant to be raised
but in dulcet song
not this matchless sudden fury-storm
words and silences like knives in my back

come away with me
lovely Athena
lie down with me in the silence
between the stars

Play

with the forms of a hundred wraiths
twisting and dancing amongst gothic pillars
flitting here and here
darting like nervous eyes
a woman in a gown silver
as the swollen silver moon
watches them in longing
pleading to waltz with them
amidst the cathedral columns and statues
she watches a moment more
then laughs and joins the wraiths in play

Phoenix Rising

beautiful sweet rhythms dancing
like flames
swaying gently calmly
hiding the passion behind motion
like a tree blowing in a yellow summer wind
soft tracing of curves
pulling grasping tasting
hard sensuality in a single glance
speaking words in volumes
silently
giving in desperately
like breathing after suffocation
consuming
consummation
conflagration
hungry flames eating dry wood
a phoenix rises from these ashes
in a startling burst of heat
this beauty
this sensual dance
is the changing of innocence to wisdom
watching motion with longing
enjoying the need
the desire
the knowledge of possession

watching graceful movement
and capturing perfect moments
locking them away within the vault of memory
storing this soul-food in tall silos
against times of heartache
these patterns are the dancing of hungry flames
leaving not cold ashes
but a phoenix rising
from the death of fire
into life

The Engines Have Ceased

engines of birth rage
in precise and loving motions
crashing in careful peals of thunder
destroying silence in lightning-laced whirlwinds
stars implode into solar storms of blue fire
everlong is defined in weird-rhythm symphonies
from my seat on nova winds
I gaze at maelstroms of making
wonderstruck at the dancing
of everycolor flames
the pistons of creation pump and punch
until voids are eaten
consumed eagerly by greenbluewhite
flickers of life

voices sing and speak to me
whisper and float to me across the ether
straining to me across the infinity of solitude
to which I am chained
I would with all my soul join this ballet
waltz to the music
so sweet and aching and distant
I would spread my arms like angel wings
soar amid the plashing morphing
dance of gods

I watch the dance beyond my reach
I look within
callow faces are seared across my memory
they are shadows
cast by figures a thousand light-years away

with these thoughts pulsing in my skull
I find myself falling like rain
through darkened skies of time
unable to cease my undulation
hurtling through mazes of eternity
I encounter there ugly foes hungry for blood
beasts of greed
and discontent
clothed in unconvincing guises
they are evil creatures
lurking in the shadows of this labyrinth
waiting for me to misstep
if I could wage war
I would march against these enemies
with phalanxes of warriors at my back
crushing resistance underfoot like eggshells
I would summon courage as my soldiers
contentment as my generals

these strange notions lose themselves
in the spaces of my skull
the callow faces frescoed god-sized
on my inner walls

become inescapable
as I wander marble temples of within
I study the visages until the pale features
are more familiar than my own

I find tears of dreaming
spilling from inner eyes
in waterfalls I cannot stop
as I weep my plummeting is stopped
by a galaxy of empty rolling hills
and there music floats to me
in whispers
I dance to the melody
tears still dripping
and I see them in the distance
The gods dancing
to the maelstrom's rhythm

the engines have ceased
the winds have slowed and died
my watching place has vanished
leaving me floating loose
like a lost red balloon
the birthing is done
I have witnessed the inception of a universe
I ride the aftermath like a tsunami
reveling in the silence of this space
that is now mine

Sequel to the Engines

I follow the trace of the dancers
till I see lightning flashing
in a distant field of nothingness
I find a seat safe from the wild thrashing
of creation-storms
watch the tango of gods
as they beautify the emptiness
I wish I could join them
the hills ring with their footsteps
the skies flash with the color of their garb
they are the engines
and their dancing is beyond me
I plead and pray
but my words are lost
swallowed by the raging of love-noises
when the catalytic motions have slowed
and stopped
I shoulder my sack of memories
follow in their wake
I belong ever in the hills watching the dance
for my feet are clumsy
my rhythm lies in my fingers
and in the temple of my skull
it is here beyond them all
that I truly exist

absorbing the flames
the winds that are nova-shards
I brush my knees and go my way
the crash of storms is done
the gods stride away
laughing as they go
leaving creation in the dust of their steps

The Singer

The skirling whirl of a traditional Irish band greeted me as I stood outside Dick O'Dow's Irish Pub. I handed the burly bouncer my ID and replaced it, entering through the propped-open green doors and into the darkened interior. The contrast between the mellow amber glow of sunset and the perpetual midnight of the pub was jarring; heavy chandeliers depended from the low ceilings, dim, orange-glowing bulbs made to look like candle flames were the only illumination besides a half dozen flat-screen TVs tuned to Sports Center. Thick, scratched, scarred wooden tables ran the length of the room opposite the bar; the tables resembled hunks of driftwood rescued from a shipwreck, retrieved and polished. The floors were ancient, scuffed weathered gray wood that seemed to have centuries of stories to tell. I remembered one of the bartenders telling me the floor planks were from an 18th century Irish hospital; I wondered what ghosts must reside silent in the whorls of the wood grain.

The band was the pièce de résistance of the pub, permeating the atmosphere with the lilting, jigging music. A tall, thin man with angular features, round, gold-rimmed spectacles, and graying hair receding in a U-shaped cul-de-sac played the penny whistle with thin, deft fingers; the fiddler was the diametric opposite, short, portly, red-bearded and long-haired, sheened with sweat as he sawed his battered, well-loved fiddle; next to the fiddler was the bodhran player, a man with fine silver hair neatly parted, an iron-gray beard closely trimmed framing patrician features, thumping his handheld drum and stomping his polished leather boots on the stage to the rhythm; last was the singer and guitar player, an elegant woman, tall and willowy, thick black hair shimmering in the dim light like raven wings.

It was her I had come to see. Her eyes were the color of moss furring a tree trunk in the afternoon sun, and she sang flawless Gaelic in a dulcet, haunting voice. I stood at the bar, ordered a whiskey on the rocks, sipped it as I watched her sway with the music. She scanned the crowd absently, strumming her guitar with red-painted fingernails. Her gaze swept across me, but didn't see me. This was reassuring.

I wasn't ready to be seen, just yet.

The bartender, who had just moments ago handed me my drink with a smile, passed by me without a glance or flicker of recognition. Moments slid past slow like sunset, and my anticipation mounted. I was growing restless, my palms damp and warm, my feet tapping a too-fast rhythm. Slow down, I told myself. Not yet.

Another whiskey, another greeting from the same bartender, as if he'd never seen me before. The set must have just started when I arrived. Damn. Impatience scoured through me; I gouged patterns in the bar top with my fingernail, deep runic shapes incised deep in the hard wood.

A third whiskey and I was burning with restless, hungry vexation. The set had to be almost over. Ah yes, now they were thanking the crowd, setting down instruments and filing out to the alley for a breath of fresh air.

I followed them out, lit a smoke, approached her with a broad smile that I hoped seemed genuine and friendly. She smiled back, shook my hand. Her palm was cool and dry, sending bolts of electric excitement through me. I caught her up in conversation, droll, mundane chit-chat. Her bandmates went back in, and I could sense her desire to end this conversation, to go with them.

It's not that easy, the fun hasn't begun yet, my lovely. Your fair, pale skin is far too perfect. I stroked the hilt of the knife in my pocket; yes, now it was time. Now.

She never saw it coming, the poor, beautiful, doomed thing.

Oh, what fun.

Her (Nightmare)

quietly droplets fall like a salt rain
unseen
nightmares flash through her
in raging patterns of hell
battering at doors
pushing at walls
inching through cracks
stealing light and snatching breath
demon forms are seen in a moment
then gone
pounding pounding pounding
like tympanic thunder or tribal drums
clothed as the beating of ghost-hearts
there and then gone
out like a candle flame
a mere memory of what it was
a bare breath
I laugh and I cry
I fall amidst the ruins of strength
lie prone in the rubble of pride
I fail despite all my love
all my efforts to rescue
crushing softness as I fall
I am only human after all
but remember always

that I will brush away the droplets of salt rain
I will soothe fears and banish nightmares
I will slay demons and douse lightning
flashing unceasing in raging patterns of hell

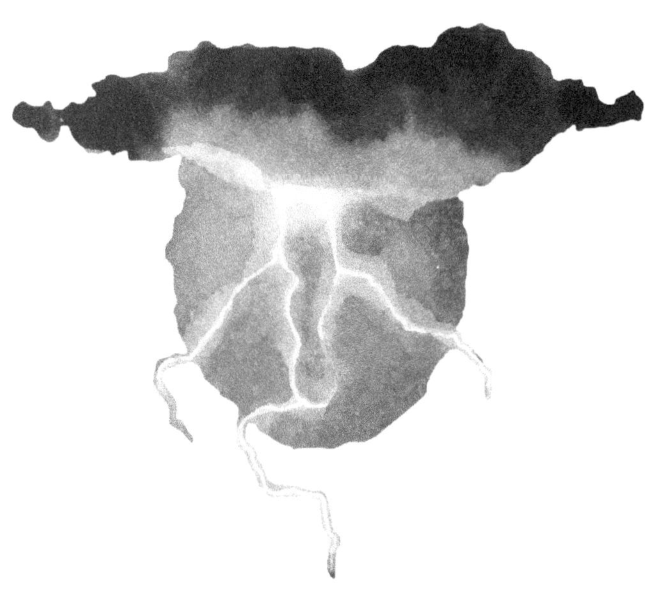

Cavern Dance

we have glass faces
translucent eyes
sight through both
as simple as looking through
our fingers trace slowly
eyebrows and chins
cheeks and lips
touching faces
searching for love
my soul waltzes to music played within
gentle but fiery
like hungry flames
when he speaks
I am set alight
my darkness is banished
like a candle burning bright
casting slow-dancing shadows
on cavern walls of within

Mayfly love

the wine goes down
along with my spirits
I sit bathed in moonglow
thinking of other bottles
glinting and gleaming
through pungent acrid smoke
laughter ringing from out of the music
thoughts and inanities bantered around
and always you and I
stealing glances and secret touches
kisses in rare moments alone
months of pent and mounting tension
culminating in that one single night
of wild ecstasy and dizzy splendor
inhibitions abandoned
deep-seated and long-rooted desires
at last given expression
in that endless too-short winter night
but then came those few sad inevitable words
exchanged slowly and quietly
reluctantly
reasons why it was mayfly love
a kind of misplaced summer romance
and now after such a long silence
so many months of violent change

I still think of you
and that night
and I wonder helplessly
what could have been

Songs to Silver Mother

Darkness enveloped us, descended upon us with slow welcome inevitability. We rose and shook and yawned and shivered and stretched, we reveled in the cool shelter night provided. We ran, weaving between quick smell-rich currents of wind and under branches thick with sighing green leaves and between tree trunks crawling with ants and echoing with earth-pulse. We dodged and nipped and yelped, we sang long high songs to Silver Mother, listened with twitching ears to answers sung by brothers and sisters on the hills and glades and peaks and dales far and near. We ran, just to run. We sang, just to sing.

We sought brother bull Moose, chased him through the wet marsh clouded with fog, ringing with frog-voice and nightingale canto. We tracked him for long hours through the night, smelling his musk, his fear-scent, our paws splashing through his wide hoofprints glinting with miniature rippling moons, we caught him at the forest edge, trapped against pond-edge, my siblings circling around behind him, my mate slinking low through the grass unseen except for eyes gleaming green through waving stalks as I distracted him with deep growls and harsh barks. We brought brother Moose to his knees and feasted on his flesh, licked our lips and sang to his spirit rising up, sang gratitude and respect for strength and cunning to lead us on the nightlong hunt. At last Bright Father began to pink the sky in the farthest places, and we trotted with full bellies through the grass and the trees and curled in our den, tangled together and contented.

We were woken abruptly by smoke. It stung our noses, drove us, pups in dangling from mouths, through the forest with panic on our tongues, terror bubbling through us as we fled from the onrushing flames. Heat pressed down and scorched our coats, the yellow orange horrible hungry fire roared and popped and ate trees and sucked the flesh from bones of slower animals, our brethren forestdwellers all around us fleeing scurrying hopping running fear bright in eyes and heaving in chests. We fled and swam the river, cowered on the other side and watched as a few failed to make the river and burst alight with rescue in view. We wept to see it, but were thankful it wasn't us. We sat on haunches and watched the forest burn, howled for our lost homes, sang for Dark Eyes and White Fur and Broken Tooth who lay in the charred soil now only scorched bones and memories beloved.

When night sank upon us once more, we sang with fervor and sorrow for lost packmates and lost homes. We sang, and we ran. We ran, sniffing new pack marks and avoided claimed territory. We ran that whole night through and the next without song, paws light and ears pricked. Just past the rising of Bright Father we found a new den, a cave in the high peaks, sat on ledges as close to the star-washed sky as we could climb, singing songs to Silver Mother as she loomed brilliant and full behind us.

Cocoon

you said it then
in the radio-filled silence
in the ache between touches

—I wish I had a bubble
not too big
just enough for us two—

and now I'm saying it
I wish I could wrap us up in this moment
weave around us a cocoon
to pause the passage of time
to deny and erase
complications and consequences
so all that exists is us
our five raging senses
merging meshing tangling
trembling together in sacred panting abandon
we would drift in that captured moment
up and away into the starwashed sky
I'm afraid of the inescapable
the bursting of our balloon
the unraveling of our cocoon
leaving us naked and weightless
and when the unpleasant and inevitable

sweeps down upon us
sweeps us apart in a flash flood of reality
I'd wrap us up and glide us away
out over the lake in a shell of you and I
and there we would tremble together
content in the eternal now
cocooned

love

it's not the clash of faces lifting in groans
suddenly freed from a prison without walls
it's not just eyes drifting and flitting
or fingers touching and twining
caressing a face leaving
it's not legs grazing under a table
touching easily then hungrily
it's not just conversation on a couch
slow or blazing into laughter
it's always mistaken for so many things
like bedsheets piled on the floor
or whispered words under the moon
it cannot be stolen
or taken
or fallen into or out of
it lives in secret places and
disappears when sought after
it will find those ready for its dizzy heights
it must be given like a Christmas gift
presented freely for the sake of itself
its truest form is disappearing
lost amid the bedsheets shared illicitly
drowned by unmeant whispers
of passion and sexuality
it is lost
but not forgotten

Shattered by Sex

His face was cold, tight, distant;
unspoken words floated in the silence
like tiny bright sparks,
fractional pieces glimmering,
scattered up from a burning whole.

—I slept with someone—
he said, dousing the silence.

I, driving, was subsumed,
swallowed by a strange calm,
a suffocating sadness.
I saw the road stretching away before me,
oddly distorted,
and I was caught up
by my own helpless flailing mind.

—Why?—
Was all I could think to ask,
in small, cold, careful words.

He stared away through the rain-spattered windshield,
a breathing sculpture of melting ice.
His tale came out in a waterfall rush,
crashing through my anger,
my unrequited love,
broken in the moment,
battered by a Niagara of flimsy excuses.

Silence flared again,
burning, scattering sparks of sentiment into the void.

—I love you still—
I whispered,
knowing much too deeply
the crushing impermanence
of such a quicksilver thing as love.

Lying all about me, then,
were the ruins of laughter and joy,
smashed and crunching beneath me
like glass and rubble.

I drove on in the smoldering silence,
shattered by sex.

The Huntress

Vi Metternich stood in front of the mirror, admiring herself. She was a tall, willowy girl of twenty-three with fine, haughty features, vivid eyes the color of blue flames, and thin, thrice-pierced lips curled in a seductive smile. She wore skin-tight black leather pants tucked in to knee-high boots studded with silver buckles and spikes, a crimson lace bustier pushing up her pale breasts to overflowing. Sheer black fingerless gloves ran up to her elbows, intricate runic tattoos showing through the gauzy material; the tattoos ran up from her palms in a serpentine spiral around her arms and over her shoulders, merged between her shoulder blades and blossomed into an intricate floral design across her entire back.

Vi struck a sensual pose in front of the mirror, chest thrust out, chin tucked down, thickly mascaraed eyelashes batting, one forefinger pressed to her mouth, pricking against a long ceramic fang where her eyetooth had been. She bared her teeth, revealing all four of the faux-vampire fangs that she had had surgically implanted three years ago, emitting a feral hiss, inch-long, black-painted fingernails splayed as claws.

"Time to hunt," she said aloud to the empty cruise ship cabin. She spun on her heel and exited the cabin, strutting down the crowded hallway with an exaggerated sway of slim hips. Anywhere else Vi would have stood out in the crowd, drawn disgusted stares and baffled glances, but this was a vampire-themed cruise, and she fit right in. The hallway was packed with people, most of them similarly attired. Vi glided through the sea of people decked out in tight leather, high boots, thick makeup (on men and women), revealing tops and scores of fangs, some implanted, some merely prosthetic; everyone was going the same direction, to the ballroom, which for this cruise was decorated with coffins and blacklights, long couches in dark corners, bars running the length of two entire walls. Couples writhed on the couches, and in some places there were more than two people tangled up in a knot of limbs and torsos like serpents locked in an ouroboros. Dubstep thumped from speakers and the dance floor was packed with grinding men and women in elaborate costumes, each more macabre and morbidly sexual than the last.

Vi lingered in the doorway, planning her entrance. There, by the bar in the furthest corner was a tall young man wearing a long, homemade cloak with a long hood thrown back to reveal boyish, attractive features that wouldn't have seemed out of place on an Abercrombie and Fitch poster. He stood against the wall, clutching a red drink—all the beverages were dyed bloodred—eyes darting around the room, upper lip beaded with sweat, weight shifting from foot to foot. He took a tentative sip of his drink, tried desperately not to splutter, coughing and hacking, drawing attention to himself that he obviously didn't want. His gaze roved over the room, stuttered, locked on Vi, who was standing with one hip cocked out, a palm planted on the swell of her backside, tousled auburn hair falling in long tangles over one shoulder, gently biting her lower lip. The boy nearly dropped his drink, openly ogling Vi, licking his lips and taking half a step forward.

Watching her prey carefully, making sure he was watching, Vi leaned over slowly, adjusting a strap on her boot, letting her breasts all but spill out in the process. Still watching him out of the corner of her eye, Vi straightened and sauntered towards him. She stopped at the bar, ten feet away. She lifted a hand and gestured to him, curling her index finger at him. The transfixed boy looked around him, as if expecting to see some other, more attractive man standing nearby. Vi shook her head and pointed at him, beckoned him again. He stumbled over to her, leaned against the bar as if the walk over had exhausted him.

Vi sidled up to him, pressed herself against him, gazed up into his limpid, nervous brown eyes. "Well hi there, sweetheart," she said in her most sultry voice, "how about you buy a lady a drink, huh?"

He nodded, lifted a hand for a bartender.

"Vodka tonic with extra lime." Vi snuck her hand around his arm, squeezed his bicep gently. "So…what's your name, darling?"

"Uh…J-Jim…."

"Jim, huh? Well, aren't you just a delicious young thing?" She took a long swallow of her drink, watching him squirm as he tried to think of an answer.

"I…am I?" he managed.

Vi traced a fingernail across his jaw, scritching on the peach fuzz, flicked him gently on his nose. "Yes, you are. Scrumptious. I could just eat you up. Devour you, you could say." As she spoke, Vi pressed even closer against him, crushing her breasts against him, curling one leg around his, a hand on his back, all but begging him to kiss her. He leaned down slightly, but she pulled away.

"Aren't you going to ask my name? It would be rude to kiss a lady without asking her name, you know."

"Uh…what…what's your name?"

"Vi."

"Vi? It's—it's nice to meet you, Vi." Vi didn't answer, just smiled, licked the vodka from her lips, took Jim by the hand. His palm was sweaty and his fingers trembled.

"Well, now. Should we go somewhere a bit…quieter? Get to know each other a little?"

"I…that would be…yeah…somewhere quieter." Jim finished his drink with a jerk.

Vi led him out of the ballroom and stopped, saying, "Which way to your room?"

Jim wiggled his shoulders in discomfort, cleared his throat, looked down at Vi. "If you want to, that is," she said, pulling away slightly. Jim looked frantic for a moment; he squared his shoulders and led her to his room, a small single in the bowels of the cruise ship.

Vi stuffed her feet into her boots, not bothering to strap or buckle them, slipped her bustier over her head and tucked herself into it. Jim lay sleeping on the bed, one arm flung over his face, twin fang-marks on this neck. Vi looked down at him with affection as she rifled his cloak for his wallet, took a couple of $20s, penned a hasty note:

Jim, sorry about the bite. It's the danger of sleeping with a vampire, you know. You're a sweet boy. You'll see me again, when you least expect it.
Don't look for me.
Vi

Alabaster and Ice

always the endless problems
you and I
drama like a soap opera
almost as if we thrive on it
we've been driven so far apart
I almost don't recognize you
for the gaping distance that looms between us
when I look in the mirror
when I look within myself
I almost don't recognize who I've become
the features are the same
but the words I hear spewing from my mouth
from yours
these are often unforgiveable
intentional knives stabbing out
I have no defense from the accusations
hurled at me like stones
I have no recourse but to fade away
without even echoing footsteps
to mark my existence
at least until I hear the fated words
please come back
but I dare not hope
for I see your anger
whirling just beneath your alabaster skin

I see the ice in your eyes
and I can scarcely dare to wish
to hope
that resolution will be so easily found

A Fantasy (Your Smile)

if I could slip up and out
of this trembling mortal coil
just for a while
I'd fly filter and slide through all the miles
from here to where to you are
I'd watch you
floating unseen nearby
just to catch a glimpse of you
to see what you do all this waiting time
this long and lonely silence between us
maybe then I'd understand a little better
be able to say all the right things
whenever you next deign to meet me
face to face
soul to soul
I'd be able to make you smile
like you once did
just for me
secrets and whispers abounding in that smile
when instead all I seem capable of
is making you wish I was gone
forever silent

Chronos

I flex my fingers and whisper sibilant words: time stops, a frozen fragment of fixed finality. I cannot save her. I can see this, and it breaks me, shatters some vital portion of my soul. I can see the bullet, a rounded, hollow-pointed thing howling towards her, seeking with awful hunger her perfect, porcelain breast; it struggles against my control, shivers, wiggles, strains forward millimeter by millimeter, and I know that it will pierce her before I can reach her. I am leaping, I am in the air reaching for her, and I will not be fast enough. I scream, and it is a guttural roar of primal rage, coming from some demoniacal portion of myself heretofore unexplored; a beast within me has been unchained, and cannot be re-caged, now.

I am not a hero, nor am I "super" in any sense of the word. I cannot fly, or bend steel, or stretch my body or shoot webs. I am merely a man who discovered a miniscule rip in the fabric of the cosmos and learned how to exploit it. It happened by sheer accident, though some may call it fate, or destiny. A scroll, a laborious translation from one dead, archaic language to another and thence into English...words read aloud, directions followed...I am a timid man, a scholar, more used to archaic hero formulae than comic book action heroes, but it seems, through this twist of fate, that I am destined to be known as Chronos, rather than James Uriah Callahan.

To tell the truth, at that moment of which I speak—when the bullet burst through my spell and splattered her crimson life-blood on the crumbling cinder-block wall—James Uriah Callahan died, and Chronos was born in his place. I have nightmares of that moment, and I wish my spells could turn back time and allow me to undo it, but if there is such a spell or power, it eludes me. I am no magician either, no wizard. What I call a spell is not really magic, nor is it a mutation or superpower. It is an incantation already ancient when the Sumerians were first learning to bake bricks, and it is limited in its use. From the instant the incantation is spoken time and the rules of physics are suspended, neither broken nor abolished, merely suspended for what I have determined is thirty precious seconds of my own personal subjective time. Anyone and anything within a fifty-foot radius is affected, and has no memory of the suspension. During those thirty seconds, I can do anything within my physical ability: I can push or pull a person, cross an intervening space, strike a blow or a fire a weapon, or simply walk away. I stop time and the rest is up to my imagination and abilities, both of which are limited.

In that first frozen moment, she is screaming, mouth in a moue of terror, hands up in a futile attempt to stop the speeding bullet, eyes half-shifted to me, pleading with me to help her, to save her. I leap with all my strength even as I finish uttering the incantation, but she is fifty feet away and I sense time beginning to reassert itself, and then with a palpable snap the tableau is broken, the bullet strikes her with a wet crunch, blood paints the wall behind her like a Rorschach image, and I slam into her a fraction of a second too late. I watch her die, then. She lies limp in my arms, eyes dimming and watery with unshed tears, breath coming in labored gasps, pink froth bubbling at the corners of her lips. She whispers my name, clutches at me, and then she is gone. I set her gently to the ground, rise up and face her killer, a hulking ape of a man with heavy shoulders and mauls for fists, one of which holds a pistol, which looks in his grip like a toy squirt gun. He has mirthful, wrathful, scornful glee in his eyes, slips the gun into his waistband at his back, spreads wide his hands, as if to say, "What are you going to do about it?" I show him. I stalk towards him, stand in front of him, glaring at him, letting my rage build, stalling for time. I am counting the seconds by the beats of my heart, and when enough time has passed, I flex my fingers again in the prescribed pattern, speak the words, loudly this time. He is puzzled, confused. The words are in a language that predates the sinking of Atlantis, and they sound like the hissing of a maddened serpent. When the last word is uttered, he is frozen, the look of befuddlement on his face comical. Now, I let loose all the cruelty and evil within me. I take the gun from his waistband, fire it point-blank into his groin, and wait for time to resume. When it does, he collapses, screaming. I kick him, stamp on his face, and then a red haze of rage washes over me and I know no more. When I come back to myself, he is a pulp of gore on the ground and she is cold and stiff, and I am covered in crusted blood.

"Layla," I whisper, finally allowing myself to feel my sorrow. She loved me, and for that she died. The dead man on the ground, he was the jealous ex who refused to let her go, who saw us in bed together and went berserk...

I leave them there, placing pennies on Layla's eyes for Charon, kissing her cold lips once more.

As I ascend the steps, I leave behind not only Layla MacPherson, but James Callahan as well. When I emerge into the star-washed midnight, I am no longer timid, or studious, or careful. I am reckless, and angry and violent.

But that formative night is not over. Stomping down the street, sparse traffic rushing by, I realize that I cannot go back to my old life, any more than I could have saved Layla. I am changed. I am altered. Do I like this new me? It is too soon to tell, I think. I am stronger, perhaps, for I care not what anyone thinks, or whether I live or die. Layla was my one love, the companion to my soul, and without her, I am naught.

I find myself wondering what havoc I could wreak with this power, what wonders I could perform. I tried to save her, and failed, but if I had been there sooner, she might still be alive. I was too late because I hesitated. I hesitated, and she died.

I wander aimlessly, distractedly, lost in my own thoughts, passing through pale pools of light and stoplights cycling green-amber-red; suddenly I find myself at the heart of downtown, deserted and silent at 3 a.m. I hear, filtering to my awareness through the fog of my self-absorption, voices nearby. A woman's voice, weeping, pleading, no no no PLEASE NO and my action is decided by motion rather than thought. I slink through shadows to the mouth of the alley from which the sounds emerge, the sound of a hand slapping a face, a whimper, a rustle of clothes, the chink of a belt buckle...

She, an unknown faceless woman who now becomes her, is lying on the rough wet cement by a reeking dumpster, pale legs flashing in the lurid sickly glow of a hanging streetlamp, and I can see her hands are tied with zip-ties and her clothes are ripped off and the man atop her is hairy repugnant vile sweating eager...

I stalk like an animal closer by inches until I am a few feet away, and the gun I never threw away is in my left hand, my right is flexing and marking the air, the words are whispered so quietly as to be subvocalization, and then he freezes mid-thrust and she freezes mid-thrash, muffled moan of protest cut short. I throw him backwards and paste his brains across the alley in gray and pink, lift her up to her feet, stiff as a mannequin, remove the underwear stuffed into her mouth as a gag, strip off my sweatshirt and slip it over her and then reality reasserts itself and she finishes her shriek, starts in shock and confusion. She looks at me, then the corpse on the ground, the ragged faded U-Conn sweatshirt that doesn't quite cover her, mumbles and stutters, falls apart weeping. I catch her, settle her down, say nothing. Eventually, she gathers herself together and asks what happened. I find no words to answer except, "I had to stop it, don't ask me how, you wouldn't believe it," and she doesn't.

I walk her to her door, a hundred feet away, shrug at her thanks, and vanish back into the night.

The next night, I wander forth, looking for trouble; I find it, easily. I try to redeem myself, moment by frozen moment, one fragment, one slice of chronology at a time. But none of it brings Layla back.

You (Escher Tangles)

You writhe and shimmer in the farthest dawn,
shredding the pale glimmers of a new sunrise,
glinting in closest focus,
hazed in distant glamour.
You tease and tantalize
my dreams and thoughts,
you push all my wants and wishes
into burgeoning grandeur.

You:
fantasies of curls and curves
against hardness and strength;
breath resounding through silence,
bodies pressed close,
pushing away emptiness.

Your intentions are unknowable
unfathomable,
You are slipping through ether;
moments and hours and lifetimes
pass us by
like river water around a boulder.
You furl and swirl though my soul
in Escher tangles,
distortion melding into clarity
and back into refraction.

Visions of us jumbled and twisted
in perfect order:
DNA,
a double-helix structure of us,
of our limbs and our skin
in wild profusion and panting abandon,
an ephemeral moment lost amid the fog,
through which are glimpsed figures
flitting and elusive,
flung about in a dance sans steps,
whose coiling motion dazzles,
collides and tumbles
with confusions and cravings.
All finally melts into the soft susurrus
of your quicksand eyes.

as the pawn falls I jump and dance
when we croon I jive inside
we crash the night through
in multicolored spirals
plashing the hues from spectrum's end to end
wading 'neath the waves
striding under a watery sun
a journey of electric composition
a symphony of crackling currents
and improbable bards
our dance spans the aeons
endures the epochs
and at the far end of infinity
we'll groove till sunrise
smiling and swilling whiskey
giggling and trickling smoke
weeping and laughing and loving sweat-slick
and when our pawn falls I jump and dance
when we croon I jive inside
I ache for your fingers
your mouth
when I find them the search is ended
and when we achieve perfection
the journey is finished
we are completed

our purpose filled
thus the opus is composed
so sing the final dirge with me
and do not weep
for even after the final line is uttered
our script continues unabated
feverish and white-hot
a wild presence felt by all
understood by none but you and me
the authors of this
our song
so sing it with me
till forever finds its end

Cavort

Calypso cavorts curvaceously
sanguine salsa dancers scintillate and scandalize
in my disordered distorted disconnected skull
hear my own thoughts reverberating
come on baby
lets tango till sunrise
sweat-slick and hard of breath
we'll scuba dive in the deeping dark of sleep
slumbering away the apocalypse
in each other's arms
we'll wake
and blue the sky will be
you and me the only ones
dancing in the phoenix light

Glamour and Silk

you stand waiting in the distance
ephemeral, nearly eternal in your mystery
your dulcet familiar voice
pierces the silent miles
years
the burnished light of your soul
lights the night in eldritch ethereal flame
your fey smile
sly evasions
beckon to me in dreams
in moments of waking fantasy
I seek you
but you slip and slither
like silk between my fingers

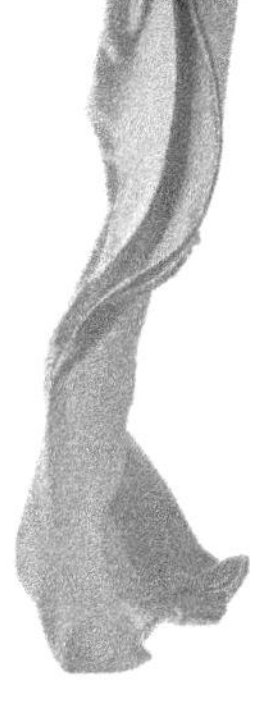

Delicious

She quickens her steps, perhaps sensing me. I know she can't see me, but I let her put some distance between us, just in case. She turns left, hunching down further into her wool coat. I drift around the corner, stop in the lee of a doorway. I watch her carefully, note when she glances behind her. She is afraid. I can smell it, feel it, taste it.

Delicious.

I shiver with anticipation. I can tell she's close to home now, nearly running, fumbling in her oversized purse for keys. She thinks home means safety. She will slam the thin hollow apartment door and turn the lock, attach the chain, breathe a sigh of relief. She might even check her windows. Then she will brew some tea, curl up on her threadbare couch and read a thick book until she falls asleep.

I know her patterns now. Night after night, I follow her home from the dingy bar where she serves watery beer to leering drunks. I come just close enough for her to sense me. She never sees me, but she can feel me. She gets gooseflesh when I'm close, her lovely pale skin pimples, the fine hairs on her neck stand up, her liquid brown eyes widen. She knows she is not alone. I breathe in the intoxicating scent of her fear. I'm close enough to touch her and her breath is shallow and quick and panting, nearly gasping, her breast is heaving, she's darting furtive glances around her, whirling in place, looking for that single scuffed step she heard, for the brush against her sleeve, the laughing male voice from an alley just behind.

Her brownstone apartment building is in front of her now, and she is up the steps and into her apartment. I wait on the landing and listen to her locking and latching. I'm in front of her door and I hear the sigh of relief. I bump against the door and she puts an eye to the peephole. Of course, she sees nothing. I am trembling, nearly unable to contain my excitement. Her nightmares have been full of red eyes and shadowy figures following her. She tosses and turns and sweats, the sheets stick to her body and she wakes with her long auburn locks tangled and damp and she is visibly terrified, alone in her apartment with the nightmares fresh behind her eyes.

I am watching her, from the fire escape. She is changing, letting stained work jeans fall to the floor in a heap, along with the shirt and underclothes. I want to go through the window and brush against her smooth bare skin, but I control myself, make myself wait for the perfect moment. She puts on a long t-shirt and curls up in her favorite spot on the couch with a blanket on her knees. The door is locked; she has checked all the windows. She is safe. She sips her tea and reads, falls asleep.

I slip through the window, careful not to rattle the glass. I keep away from the sharp line of light slicing between door and frame, watch her sleeping. I slide through the narrow gap, creep closer. A picture frame rattles as I pass by. She stirs, but doesn't wake. I am above her now, she can feel me even past the oblivion of slumber; her skin pimples, she shudders and tugs the blanket higher. I let out a long sigh that knocks over the mug and rustles the pages of a magazine. She hears it, this time. Her eyelids twitch and flutter open. Freshly woken, the filters of perception haven't blinded her yet: she sees me. For a moment she is too startled and confused to react, then she pulls in a lungful of air and screams. The dulcet delicious sound of her terror ripples through me in a bolt of pure pleasure. I swirl in circles, moan in ecstasy, shiver like a wave-distorted reflection. I swell through the dimensions, burgeoning from the influx of her fear. She screams yet louder. I course around her in uncontrollable paroxysms and she is scrambling off the couch and crawling across the floor, t-shirt rucked up around her naked hips. I follow her, wait for her to close her bedroom door, I push through it, laughing and howling. She is huddled between bed and wall, staring at me through her tears.

"What do you want?" she begs, voice tremulous.

I don't answer. I writhe closer, brush against her, feel the warmth of her. I stretch around her, absorb her heat, her terror.

Delicious.

"What do you want?" she asks again, shrill and panicked.

I don't answer. I plunge forward and down in through her open mouth and I am in, I am here, I have taken her now, possessed her, and I boil into every smallest space of her soul. She shrieks as she feels me filling her up like bile, feels me welling within her in an inexorable surging that she cannot stem and the shrieking is changing, turning into a moan, a gasp, a denial, a desperate refusal to accept that she likes this, she wants this, oh yes, but she doesn't want to want it. She hates her own desire. I can feel her thinking now, her thoughts run over the surface of our mind, she is casting last glances around as she slowly relinquishes control to me like drowning. She sees a crucifix and I panic just a little as she reaches for it. I delve deeper into her will and twist, just so, bring forth pleasure, bring forth heat in just the right places, in the just the right amount. She writhes and forgets the crucifix, collapses to the floor and abandons herself to me. Her choked moans are equal parts terror, ecstasy and desperation. She is sobbing and heaving and moaning, and she is all mine, all mine.

Delicious.

Lovely Beast

you swirled in
a coriolis wind
pregnant with memories and emotions
words spoken
desires tamped down by time
now roiling just beneath the surface
all these meld and merge
struck by lightning touch of lips and fingers
now the thin skin of resistance
reasons why not
burgeons and bursts
passion is birthed
erupting full and furious
trailing skeins of truth
pulled free in knotted lines
sentences calm and heavy

we shift away
try to ignore
that lovely beast between us
hungry and hesitant
try to pretend we aren't matches lit
in a room full of explosives
then a single fateful spark
a brush of knees

a bulging pause and locked eyes
and we can't pretend anymore
we are consumed
kiss ignites into sweeping wildfire
and we're sweetly desperately drowning
neither you nor I want to surface
gasp air
douse the flames
we want to burn hotter
dive deeper

but the reasons why not raise their heads
so familiar is this feeling between us
it was me back then
and it's you now
so much else freighted in the years between
and the whole time the radio plays softly
rending refrains speaking to our dilemma
choruses echoing our tortured hearts

it's cold outside
the freezing razor edge of winter
even that cannot cool the fire between us
we share a cigarette and huddle close
not daring to touch
lest we reignite our chaotic Shakespeare love
You leave in the small dark hours
between midnight and dawn
an apt metaphor describing you and me

stuck midway between one and the other
so much more and so much less
no way back and no way forward
you leave with a single soft glance behind
so full of things unsaid
smothered with tamped desires
the fire now banked to coals

but we both know all too well
the power of a single touch

Wings and Faces

I tire of this waiting game
Angel
you have come and gone
waiting now somewhere far from me
waiting for me to find you
hiding behind the curtain
of some unknown night
if I could grow wings
and fly away to search the farthest skies
the very star-burned heavens
for your calm brilliant face
I would beat those wings with all my strength
bend trees like grass
with hurricane winds
if I could take the face
of every woman man and child
disguising myself so I could hide near you
close enough to smell your beauty
to feel the breeze of your passage
watching as you smile
brighter than the silver moon
if I could do these things
fly with angel wings
morphing into each face near you
I would

I would crash the distance through
to hold you in my arms
and I would catch each face until I found you
Angel
wherever you now hide

Bathsheba

I cannot get her out of my head.

She haunts me, waking and dreaming. I see her in that one momentary vision, stolen and hoarded away in my soul. I see the copper basin, plain and unadorned, each hammer dent visible. The basin is large and full of steaming water, sitting in a pool of sunlight in a courtyard, surrounded by date palms and ferns, lilies and jasmine. I see the maidservant pour the last bucket of heated water into the basin and curtsy to someone just out of view. I am standing on a private rooftop at the edge of my palace where it borders the homes of the modestly wealthy; I am alone in the palace except for a few servants. I see her now, she has approached the basin and is standing next to it staring off into middle distance as she lets down her hair from its elaborate braid. Her hair spills down in long black waves, shimmering in the bright morning sunlight, deep lustrous black like raven's wings, like a starless night. Her shift is white, pure, spotless linen, so finely woven as to be nearly translucent, pressed by a slight breeze against her body, young and lush and nubile.

I stand in my courtyard and watch her, spying, feeling the guilt burn in my chest, tangling with desire and excitement. I stand and watch her, unable to turn away, knowing I should. She leans over and dips a hand in the water, lifts a cupped palmful, watches the drops fall and I can see the prism reflection as the sun catches them and they shine like slow-falling diamonds, splashing down to send ripples running to the edge. She shrugs out of her shift and lets the material fall gently to the marble tile at her feet in heap around her delicate ankles. She stands bare in the sunlight, unashamed, thinking herself alone and unwatched.

I was transfixed, hypnotized by her beauty.

Her skin was flawless and tanned, her flesh firm, her breasts high and full and swaying slightly as she stepped away from the shift piled on the tile floor. She stood with her arms crossed over her chest, her head turned to look over her shoulder with her weight back on one leg, the other slightly bent. She stood for several moments in that pose of feminine grace, just long enough to burn the memory in my mind for all time, then she stepped into the basin and sat down, dipped her head backward into the water, back arched in a parabola, her hair spreading in the water like an ink stain on pure white parchment. She bathed herself slowly, leisurely, enjoying the warmth, calling once for more hot water, luxuriating in the day's dawning brilliance. I watched her the entire time, feeling all the while a hot burning pit of shame searing my soul. At last she rose and toweled herself off and stepped back into her robe, the thin material clinging to her still-damp skin, tantalizing me yet more. Then she was gone from view and I felt a hollowness within me, a burgeoning hunger in my gut for that woman, that vision of perfection, the epitome of womanhood.

I returned to my chamber, slumped into a chair and called for strong wine, not even acknowledging the servants as they bowed, exiting. The day was long, full of images of the woman I had seen, consuming my attention so that I gave little thought to the business brought before me. By day's end I was nearly feverish. I had to have her. I fought against it with all my strength, but found myself powerless against the tide of desire that was sweeping away my good reason.

Wine clouded my sight and my mind as I flopped to my bed and fell into a restless, dream-shattered sleep. I dreamed of her in a thousand scenes, but the one dream that has stayed with me, to this day, is also a dream that haunts with its vividness, its lurid reality. I woke, in the dream, from a drunken slumber tangled in sweat-sodden sheets to see her in the doorway of my chamber, outlined by flickering torch light. She came to me in the dream, swaying seductively towards me, hair loose and gleaming. She untied the neck of the shift so that the V of her breasts showed silver in the moon-light streaming in from the open window, shrugged off the shift in a lithe, sensual movement, sending shivers down my spine. She came over to me and put a hand to my face, eyes large limpid pools of soil-brown, pressed herself against me. I reached up a hand and ran it down the curving line of warm silken skin from strong legs like pillars, to hips full and firm to the swell of her breast to the hollow at her neck, where I placed a soft and gentle kiss…

And then I woke up, alone, sweating, chest heaving, a gut-wrenching sense of loss ripping through me.

I ached. I was filled with longing, overcome by obsession…

These dreams, these awful, sweet fantasies, they are nearly nightmares, now. Days have passed, filled to saturation with dreams and thoughts of her. I wake soaked in sweat, steeped in a pall of all-consuming obsession that I cannot contain, that I know will lead me to sin.

God, help me. I am bewitched. Waking or dreaming, I have but to close my eyes and I am whisked away to some far pasture bathed in the sun, a lush green valley ringing with birdsong and eagle cry, sheep bleating softly and a breeze blowing, the grass waving their million hands heavenward. She is there with me in that place, resting against my chest as we lie in the shadow of a tree, wine-muzzy and love-sated, content and alone. The heavy weight of the crown is set aside, the burden of the nation is lifted, if only for an afternoon.

My mind races and my blood boils, caught up in the burning web of that fictive memory. I lie awake all night, tangled in sweat-soiled sheets, my forehead fevered in the coolth of my marble hall; I am restive, restless, reckless. I pace my room furiously, waging a war in my soul.

I *must* have her. I *must*. I am king, I cannot be

refused. She will be mine, and no alternative will be countenanced.

Servants bring word that her name is Bathsheba. Bathsheba. They say also that she is married to a soldier, a Hittite named Uriah. My desire and my guilt wage a heavy and fearsome war within me, and I fear my righteousness shall be defeated.

She comes! I have sent messengers to bring her to me. It won't be long now, and I will have this woman, this treasure. My limbs tingle with anticipation, my brow is sweating. I pace my throne room restlessly, a lion in a cage, silent on massive padded feet, crossing and recrossing, roaring and rumbling as it stares out between the bars of its prison.

She stands now in the doorway of my throne room, garbed in a simple, becoming dress of green linen, inexpensive but tightly fitted, clinging to every curve. My mouth goes dry at the sight of her, my groin tightens with desire. I clench the armrest of my throne so tightly I hear the wood creak under my grip. She approaches the dais, timid and confused. Her long black hair is loose around her shoulders, her head covered by a piece of cloth that matches her dress. She kneels before me, head down. I can see her hands trembling.

"You sent for me, my lord King?" Her voice is low, musical.

"Rise, come here." It is difficult for me to speak.

My voice is thick, my words come slowly, my breaths are long and deep. She rises, climbs the dais, lifts her eyes to mine, hesitantly, then more boldly. I can see in her eyes that she is confused, but unafraid. She stands barely a foot away now, and I stare at her greedily, hungrily. She returns my gaze, and I see comprehension dawning on her face.

I rise from my throne, take her hand in mine, lead her to my chamber, dismiss the servants. Her hand is warm and dry, steady. She knows what is happening. She doesn't resist, doesn't speak a word of refusal. I've seen the look in the eyes of servant girls when the soldiers take them their rooms: some of them go willingly, their eyes shimmer with eagerness, others, those with husbands or lovers go less willingly, and I can see in those eyes the unspoken "no" clear and apparent. I turn my head to look at Bathsheba, and I see no demurral in her eyes. She must see the question in my eyes, for she squeezes my fingers, lifts her head proudly.

We arrive at my chambers and I sit on the bed. She stands before me, and I am burning like a torch, more alive than ever, as full of life and energy as before a battle. My vision, my fantasy, the dreams that have haunted me for a week are becoming reality. She reaches for me, pulls at my belt, removes my tunic. The afternoon sunlight streams in through a window, bathes her in a pool of gold as she undresses. I can see lust beginning to well up in her eyes, in the shallow panting of her breath, in the way she leans over me, circles her arms around my neck.

Her breath smells of mint, her hair of jasmine.

The moon is high and the stars bright when she leaves me. I walk to her to a postern gate not far from her own doorway. She kisses me, briefly, like a lightning bolt.

"What now, my lord king?"

"I will send for you." She curtsied, darted across the street and was gone into the shadows.

I stood there in the street, concealed in a shadow, for a long time, watching the moon descend slowly, thinking.

A servant hands me a slip of parchment folded into quarters. I unfold it, read the single line written in a neat, feminine hand.

I am pregnant.

I fall back against my throne, panic welling in my stomach like bile, now it grips my heart, now is rising to burn my throat. She is with child?

What have I done?

A plan takes shape and I call for writing materials and a fast messenger. I pen a note to Joab, telling him to send me Uriah, the husband. Her husband. I suppress guilt as I watch the rider bear the note eastward to Rabbah.

Uriah arrives, dusty from travel, a bandage around his arm, spotted red with blood. He is tall, dusky, unattractive. He has a hard face, his eyes tell of many battles, his scars tell a story of an accomplished fighter. I ask him how the siege of Rabbah fares, and Joab. He describes the battle in short, succinct statements, little imagination or poetry to his descriptions, just the details and facts of a lifelong soldier. I send him home to wash his feet, send him gifts as a mark of my favor. Servants tell me that he refused to go home, sleeping instead with the servants.

I summon him and he explains: "The ark and Israel and Judah dwell in booths, and my lord Joab and the servants of my lord are camping in the open field. Shall I then go to my house, to eat and to drink, and to lie with my wife? As you live, and as your soul lives, I will not do this thing."

I grudgingly respect this man, this poor doomed soldier. He is honorable, courageous, determined. What must be done, must be done. He stays with me for two more days, at my insistence. We drink skinfuls of wine, share war stories, compare scars and sword techniques. I can sense him beginning to question his presence with me, however. At the end of the second day, I send him back to Rabbah with a letter for Joab:

Set Uriah in the forefront of the hardest fighting, and

then draw back from him, that he might be struck down and die.

Word came, a month later. Uriah was dead, fallen valiantly in battle. I send for Bathsheba, and I tell her myself.

"Your husband is dead."

To lessen the blow? Perhaps.

She stands shocked for many long moments, her lovely face blank. She sinks down to her knees, tears her garment down the middle. Even in her visible grief, my lust warms. She laments loudly, returns to her home to observe the period of mourning. When the mourning is done, I send for her again, and she comes to me.

We lie in my bed, drowsing and talking of such things as lovers do, after. She lifts up on an elbow, her hair a curtain of black against her skin, against mine. Her eyes presage a hard question.

"Did you do it, David?" Her eyes demand truth.

I know what she is asking me. I cannot deny her this. I cannot meet her eyes as I struggle to admit it to her.

"Yes." The single word of affirmation sits heavily between us. I force myself to say it all, to put it in words. "I sent him to the siege at Rabbah. He fought like a wounded lion, I am told. He was struck by arrows taking the gate. He died like a man, like an honorable warrior."

"Why? Why me?"

"I saw you bathing, once. From that balcony, there. I saw you, and I had to have you. And I now I do." She is at a loss for words. "Did you love him?"

She thinks carefully before answering. "He was a good man. Kind, in his way."

"You did not answer the question."

"It was a marriage made by my father, when I was more girl than woman. I learned to care for him, in time. He took care of me, he was gentle with me. He was a warrior, though, through and through, and the son of a warrior. Tenderness, affection, gestures of love were... unlike him. And there were many battles far afield, in service of my lord. There were many days spent alone."

I feel something sharp bite my spirit. Guilt, that ravening beast, lurks within. I push it away, bear up under the pang until it subsides. I turn to her, take in her beauty, and I forget the beast within.

She bears me a child, a son. He is as lovely and perfect as his mother.

Nathan, the prophet, has come to me. He stands before me, tall, strong, dark from days in the sun, work-rough hands, hair long and wild and his eyes full of fury, righteous anger. He tells me a story of a rich man with many sheep who steals the single ewe lamb that belonged to a poor man. I become angry at the avarice of the rich man, until Nathan tells me that *I* am the rich man. He rails against me, reminds me of all that the Lord has given me. The Lord God of Israel speaks to me, from Nathan's mouth. I hear His words, and I feel the guilt I have been denying, that I have been hiding in my heart, and it wells up within me, a tide I cannot any longer hold back. It overtakes me, squeezes my heart until it cracks.

At Nathan's last words, it breaks:

"Nevertheless," he says to me in a voice heavy and sepulchral, "because by this deed you have utterly scorned the Lord, the child who is born to you shall die."

He pins me to my throne with his piercing, penetrating gaze, then turns away and leaves, abandoning me to my guilt.

The child, my precious baby, has died. I can even now, as I sit in a darkened room, weeping, hear the child piteous cries, weak with fever. I pleaded with the Lord, fasted, lay on the ground and begged Him to spare the child and punish me, but after seven days, seven long, endless days of agony and guilt, the child died. It was nameless, buried in a shallow grave under a tree in a palace garden.

Bathsheba lies in our bed, alone. The pillow is wet with tears, her lustrous hair is tangled and matted, a heavy curtain blocks the sunlight, closing her in with her pain. It breaks my heart further to see her thus. I go in to her, lie down next to her, take her lovely face in my spear-roughened hands, kiss her deeply.

"Will God give us another baby, David?" Her eyes glisten, search mine. I do not know, and I cannot speak to say so. She senses my doubt, weeps against my shoulder.

I stand on a balcony, look down into a courtyard. My son, Solomon, sits in the dust next to a splashing fountain. I watch him as he struggles to his feet, wobbles, balances, toddles to Bathsheba, chubby arms outstretched. I feel joy spring up in my heart, welling up like the fountain below. The deep waters of joy, however, are salted with the knowledge of the child who is not here, who should be sitting on Bathsheba's lap as little Solomon learns to walk, laughing and clapping perfect little hands.

Bathsheba turns and looks up at me, sensing my presence. She smiles at me. Motherhood has made her lovelier still, but I can see in her eyes the sorrow for our lost baby.

Myth #1

fireflies wink blink flash
light up your face watching mine
fireflies blink blink blink
a mating dance to match the two of us
dancing round the edges of love
fireflies flash like stars floating about us
solar system in yellow miniature
lighting up sparks between us
let's go back inside
let the fire die
leave the dancing fireflies to mating rituals
while we mate and dance and love

My Sweetsweet Him

a gobbet of disaster hits smackdab
in the middle of tomorrow
as if those high high walls weren't there
for the protection of our tomorrows
cement squares pass underfoot
smoothslow and trolling lazily along
for the sake of it being night right now
without a care for the humid air
clouding around us like bathroom steam
after a midmorning shower
swirling all around my finally yes
(IHOPEITHINKIPRAY)
sweet him

boating slowly updownup
in the storm-mad Pacific
waves world-high
clinkclinkclinkclink of sail on mast
my taskmaster him shouting at the storm
or is it me
me
ME
always me
as if he were some kind of tabby or calico
and I his scratching post

ME
wishing wet and cold never existed
wishing he or I never existed

a gobbet of disaster detonates nearby
a grenade of sudden shards and shrapnel
still sticking in my unseen body
(MINDHEARTSOUL)
(un)sweet him
injecting my corrupted no longer innocent body
goodbye goodbye
(GODLETMENOTBEDREAMING)

poetry and whispers soft and him
tall sunshine
my own lover
him
a different him
not taskmaster him
my sweetsweet him
passing the concrete caravans underfoot with me
strolling late at night
past churches at midnight
erasing the ihateyou's (unactually spoken but real)
the deaths in mind
and even tried once or twice and failed
(THANKGOD)

so spilled I my inner milk

the liquid of my soul
into a wishlover cup
a handsome face
and waiting hands
looking back now at then
old and happy
maybe not methuselah
but wiser and lover-filled
and it seems those long ago years
of taskmasterhim-filled hell
were but some awful dream
wafted up from an otherwhere
a hades place
reeking with the stench of the inky styx

thoughts of that long ago then
fill me with hate and bile and tears
and thoughts of this now
and my sweetsweet him
fill me with contentedness
the mercurial rain from the eyes of my
(THANKYOUGODTHANKYOU)
sweetsweet him
so full of Iloveyou
A him puzzle-made for me

Starlessness

it's a kind of darkness
birthed fully formed and furious
born without knowledge of light
under the black of a moonless starless sky
no old familiar orbits or constellations
no knowledge of what was
nothing born of nothingness
this is strange and unfamiliar
like the taste of blood to a newborn
alien but tasting vaguely of déjà vu
every breath in
the darkness is a lungful
every breath out
the darkness recedes
a battle of sorts without a winner
or even weapons
kindle a flame in the silence
keep it low and flickering
like a last breath preserved for an infinity
for a time of breathlessness yet to come
the flame inside threatens me
waiting and lurking and hiding
like a thief in the night
creeping in through an open window
on a starless night

the absence of stars is a phenomenon
the unsalted sky is an omen
stargazers fear to see
the heaviness of the heavens
empty
gaping like the inside of a velvet bag
they expect to see a bold expansive canopy
flaunting millions of ticks and flecks
and washes of light
dazzling the drowsy cold-slapped eyes

the confusion inherent in all this
is a desire for something seen
but never felt
heard but never voiced
consoled but never needed in turn
the heaviness
the cold and starless sky
all this is a vivid symbol
a kind of allegory
a riddle to be solved
and the only clues
are desire
and chains

Voice of the Tempter

I feast on the dreams of the broken
Salivate over their silent misery
I prowl on wicked paws through the wreckage of joy
My lair is a nest of fear and doubt
Give me more agony
More turmoil
I glut on the shivers of the weeping
When weakness opens the veins of the sinful
Then I slip in, slow and smooth and silent
A narcotic high of whispers and needling murmurs

I am the tempter

I cannot be killed
For I am nothing you can fight
Just the voice of doubt
The whisper of temptation

I am the the murmur in your gut,
saying "you'll never amount to anything"
The voice muttering in the moment of desire,
"It wouldn't be so bad, would it?"
I am the jealousy
The anger over minor hurts and inconveniences
The doubt that you could ever be enough
When you feel like you've sinned so badly

that you doubt if you're still saved...
That's me, too
When you sink into sorrow,
Delve into despair,
Give into grief,
And cannot find the mercy and joy of
The One
That's me

You cannot defeat me
I prowl the earth
Roar and exult in the moments of despair

You cannot defeat me
Not on your own

Don't call on His name
Don't you dare seek His help
You don't deserve it
You've done too many dark, vile things
Those secret sins?
He sees them
You think you're forgiven?
Like it could be just that easy?
I know what you've done.
I tempted you to do it.
I pulled you into the pit of despair,
Rejoiced when you gave into my temptation
Instead of praying.

You can't defeat me.
You can pray all you want…
He's not listening.
He has too many other prayers to answer.
More important matters to attend.
You're nothing.
He doesn't love you that much.
He can't love you, not with all you've done.
How could He forgive THAT?

Keep praying.
Go ahead.
See how effective it is.
He doesn't answer.

Your prayers are empty.
There's no power in His Name.
No power in His Blood.
It wasn't shed for the likes of YOU.

Pray all you want.
I'll be back.
I'll tempt you again.
Whisper my poison in your ear.
When you're caught in the jaws of depression,
I'll be there.
You can pray my voice to silence all you want,
Turn to Him until I must flee,
But I'll be back.

Us

calm pressing pulling pushing
urgent flight without motion
screaming and singing in the vacuum of space
waltzing through time
all down and up and out and in
clasping grasping clutching hands
pressing lips to lips
but only for a moment stolen
wishing for the next fragment of passion
hoping for it to rush in on stealthy feet
or sweep everything away in hurricane winds
waiting for reality like dreaming
thoughts burning
like flames licking at paper edge
trickling and crawling slowly along
until the whole is raging
like anger
consuming hungrily desperately
as if there could never be enough
brilliant changing pulsing musical enveloping

Soulward

a fire flickers and wavers
a silence deep
breathless and porcelain
burgeons soulward
my eyes open slowly
a fire inside me trembling
I await
him

Mad Mary

The air smells of lunacy. Smell it? Delicious. Lovely, wafting to the nostrils like Mom's apple pie. Tasty, she was. The madness has a distinct olfactory punch to it that cannot be mistaken. It's not like fear. Fear smells thick, like spilled blood. Madness is light, almost frilly, delicate and thinly pungent.

Ah, yes. There she is. What'ssssss her name? Mary? Yes, that's it. I lean in to the outskirts of her mind and listen:

The cows come home home home, all day all day... where mind the gallows go, inclines declines...algorithms of alcohol...

I withdraw, leave her to her nonsense chanting. She's pressed far past the bounds of what can be understood as thought, much less coherence. Perrrrrfect.

She mumbles and stumbles, swigs from a brown paper bag in the shape of a bottle; I flare my nose and sniff...King Cobra, I think...yes, yes. She's far gone, too. Many bottles in, this day.

"Periwinkle, twinkle twinkle little star, how I wonder who you are..." she weaves around a corner and into an alley, lurches to a stop, inspects her surroundings, sinks and sags to the ground in a pile of newspapers and cardboard arranged into a nest, still whispering to herself in a barely audible sing-song "it's contagious, here we are now, imitate us..."

Nirvana? Really, Mary? Ah the mad, no taste whatsoever.

I wait, wait, wait, tasting the shadows, watching the stars come to life beyond the cloud cover. Night falls; Mary sleeps. The crowds fade, and no one sees me. They never do. I disguise myself as something living, something real. Something vaguely human, or human shaped. I love their ignorance, these frail, mad humans.

Finally, the moment comes, and I strike like an adder, swift and silent. She tastes of madness, so sweet like honey-wine and anger, acrid like aged scotch. When I finish with her she is a flaccid sack of nothing, but I sense her soul wafting upward like a smoke trail and she is relieved, thankful. She whispers to me, before she vanishes among the waiting multitudes of the In-Between—

Thank you thank you, death is like loving—

I smile a toothy grin and slither back into the cool shades of nowhere.

Half-Demons and Angel-Ghosts

livid scars of voices gash themselves
across the flesh of silence
the thin skin of solitude is torn
these voices pound in my brain
haunting my thoughts and dreams
angel-ghosts dancing in my skull
floating in my soul
they have found me
for I created them
the voices whisper of what was
they describe in hushed voices an aching history
I know these voices
these whispering half-demons
they are us
me and you my love

Maybe

Maybe my words sound all too familiar;
I know he said them.
Maybe he held you the way I do;
I know he must have, at least once.
Maybe my hands bring back
the ache of his on you,
and maybe my kiss on your lips
is all too familiar,
reminding you of all the times he tried;
I know it must.

I see this all in your eyes
that I get so lost in,
the way he never did.
Maybe hearing me say
"I love you,"
hurts like hell,
because he said that too.

Maybe your innocence is gone,
taken when he raped you,
every night, every day,
every time he touched you,
staining you inside and out,
with his words, with his hands;
I know he did.

I know you're scared,
but maybe you don't have to be:
I'm not him.

Staining Silver

for hours sat the glass, unbreakable
a silent eye looking far and wide
looking years unending
for a ghost, an angel

for hours sat the glass, unbreakable
waiting an eternity with fairy tales of love
glinting in the reflections of its face
like the sky turned liquid

for hours sat the angel, broken
a sweet-faced seraph
the ballad of her soul glinting in her tears
pooling on the polished tile
wetting her gown and staining her toes
silver

to the towertop ascends the angel, porcelain
a storm-torn seraph
climbing stone stairs
spears of sunlight
shining through painted windows
leaving her tears on the cobblestone
like glass drops
wetting the floor and staining the stairs
silver

there in the tower sits the angel and the glass
one broken
the other unbreakable
tears of the angel still fall
wetting the floor and staining the glass
silver
shattering the unbreakable
shards falling like sharpened rain

out of the rubble comes a prince
prisoner of time
his savior an angel
a storm-torn seraph
porcelain stained silver

together they descend the tower
slipping on pools of glass
tripping on shards of silver
fleeing out into eternity

No Eye Is On the Sparrow

There is no one to see this scene; the entire world is empty and silent, it seems. The whisper of wingtips is a loud sound, and the cheery trill of sparrowsong is louder still.

The sparrow is old.

One does not think, often, of birds and mice and wild things as being young or old, as living creatures that age. Glance out the window, right now, this moment: see that bird twittering and wheeling? Such wild creatures, the small ones that fill the spaces of nature, the insignificant ones, they go unnoticed.

This sparrow, singing innocent soaring songs, is old. It has seen days come and go, has hatched eggs and guided first flights, has made new nests and sang to the sunrise. It sits on a frail, slender branch, a shoot so near the top, so delicate that the merest breath of wind sends it swaying to and fro. The sparrow clings with tiny-clawed feet, singing to no one.

Then its song slows, ceases. The wind falls silent. Clouds cover the sun.

The sparrow falls.

Its feet let go of its perch and its aged wings cannot catch the air, cannot bear it back aloft. It hits the grass with an inaudible thump; wings splay limp, feet curl and droop. The sparrow sees with fading sight the spinning, trackless blue, once its aerial home, now far and unreachable. The clouds clear and a breeze rattles the oak branches, stirring stilled feathers, snatching and cradling and carrying away a final trilled note of farewell.

Silence reigns, now.

No eye is on the sparrow, but it does not pass on alone.

A Farewell Silence

The loft was cold, dark and quiet in the predawn hours. The man lay on his back, one arm underneath his head, covered to the waist by a sheet, a woman next to him on her side facing away from him, hands underneath her cheek.

Neither was asleep. The pillow by her face was damp, her brown eyes glittering with slowly trickling tears; the man, thin and hard-muscled with black hair touched by silver at the temples, sighed. It was a long deep sorrowful expulsion of breath that spoke of grief, wordless and knife-sharp.

"Maybe we can—" he began to say.

"No," she cut in. "I can't…I just can't go through that again." She shook her head gently.

"Well, maybe we can just wait a few months, and then when we—when you—feel ready, we can try again."

The woman rolled over to face him, laid a thin delicate long-fingered hand on his chest, familiar and loving. "No. I'm sorry. I…I just can't." Her face was like her hands, thin, delicate, beautiful in a fragile, angular way. "Please try to understand, Mark. I've wanted this more than anything, to be able to give you this. I know how much it means to you. I love you, so much. I just…couldn't bear to lose another one."

He reached his free hand up and pinched the bridge of his nose, wiped his face as if trying to scrub the riot of emotions away. "Melanie…" He turned his head to look at her, hard sad features softening. "I know. I shouldn't even ask you to. I couldn't bear to lose another one either. I feel like something has been torn out of me. Like I was given my deepest desire and had it snatched away again." His composure crumpled abruptly and he rolled away from her, digging the heels of his palms into his eyes, almost savagely.

Melanie shifted closer to him, pressing herself against the length of him, wrapping an arm around him. "I feel the same way, believe me. More so, if anything."

"I know," he said, heaving another deep shuddering sigh. "I know. It's just not fair. Why us? When there's so many people out there who don't even appreciate what they've been given? They take it for granted, like it's so easy."

There was silence for a long time, then. Finally, Mark rolled over to his back once more and she laid her head on his chest. "So that's it then," he said slowly. "I feel like I'm saying goodbye to someone, you know? Someone I've never met…never will, now."

"Please…don't talk like that. It's not fair. You know all too well how to get me all twisted around, talking me into things, arguing and turning things upside down, and making it all so…dramatic and…final, I guess."

"Isn't it though? Dramatic? And final?"

"Well, yeah, I guess so. I just feel like when you talk like that that you're trying to persuade me into trying again, without sounding like you are."

"I'm not, I promise. I'm not gonna lie though. I do wish we could try again, but I know, in practical terms, that neither of us can emotionally endure all this again…the joy at first, the hope, the excitement of the plans and buying tiny little clothes in blue or pink, and cribs and diaper bags and…and then the agony when you lose it…him…or her…that unbearable, wrenching pain of loss…"

"Oh Mark…" she sobbed against him, shoulders shaking.

"I'm sorry, I have to get this out, Melanie," he said, his voice low and heavy, barely controlled, tremors and trembles at the edges. "I'm the last of my family, you know? Dad died last year, Mom when I was a kid… they were both only children, and their parents were gone before they even met each other. I have no one but you—I just want to leave a legacy, a baby to carry on some part of me. It doesn't even have to carry on my name, I just want some portion of myself to go out into the world. I feel like if I die some spark will be extinguished. You have your brothers and sisters, and nephews and nieces, and your mom and dad and everyone…but you're all I have. I can't risk you again, I can't—there was so much blood last time, I thought I was gonna lose you and I couldn't survive that. If I lost you I'd just stop breathing, heartbroken and dead inside. But I've wanted a baby for *so long…*"

"I know you have…and I've tried so hard to give a baby to you. We've tried everything Mark, and we've lost them all. This time was the worst, making it to twenty weeks…And it gets worse every time for me, physically."

"I'm not blaming you. How could I? I know you want this as much as I do. I guess I'm just grieving, because I know we just have to give up." He groaned, a ragged growl of heartache. He didn't say anything for a long time.

"I'm saying goodbye," Mark said, finally.

Melanie couldn't respond, she could only clutch harder to him, kiss him through her tears. Outside, the sun had fully risen, welcoming a new day. The loft was quiet then, filled with a farewell silence.

In the Zoo

They'd taken me on a bright, cloudless day. It had been hot, and still. They came down from the sky in a whirring, humming, sleek silver craft, descending in a sudden rush and flare, flattening the grass. I hadn't hidden, or run.

They were clothed in material that shimmered with a translucent energy, a silvery glow like moonlit mercury obscuring their features entirely.

Looking back, now, I wish I had run. I was afraid, of course, paralyzed with fear.

They subdued me with laughable ease, three of them. The one in the center lifted a hand—four fingers, and a thumb—flicked a wrist, a pushing gesture, a contemptuous motion. I was gripped by an invisible fist, a crushing force that bound my arms against my sides, slammed me to the ground. I could neither move nor speak, and the fist was slowly squeezing me, pressing in on my lungs, cutting off my breath, forcing my vision into a shrinking tunnel. Then the pressure eased and I could breathe. I was on the verge of passing out, holding myself on this side of consciousness by dint of helpless rage and morbid curiosity. One of the figures bent over me, placed a circular disk on my chest; I felt weightless, as if I was perpetually falling. If I could have moved, I would have flailed and kicked; if I could have made a sound, I would have screamed. As it was, I could do nothing but let them push me, guiding me to their ship like a shopper pushing a cart.

One of them leaned over me, touched a finger to my forehead, and I was swallowed by sleep.

When I awoke, I was in a cell, about eight feet high, ten feet wide, and twenty feet long. The four walls were made of the same shimmering mercury as my captors' suits, except these walls were translucent. I was lying on a cot, thin and hard, covered by a rough woolen blanket. In one corner were two large metal bowls, water in one and one with a cold gruel.

I stood and approached one of the walls, reached out a hand, tentatively touched the substance, felt a burst of cold followed by a shock that tossed me across the cell and into the other wall, which absorbed and held me, turned rock hard, dumped me to the floor, moaning and cursing.

It was dark beyond the walls. I could make out a few shapes, all large rectangles about the same size of my own cell. The shapes were arranged around me in a wide circle, mine in the very center.

I sat on the cot and waited, as there was nothing else to do. I thought of my dog Marlow, a German Shepherd, and my girlfriend Julie, who was dumping me and moving out. I had been walking in Central Park when they took me, clearing my head after an argument, working through what to say to get Julie to stay.

The park had been eerily empty. It was just past noon, on a Tuesday in March. I had $300 on the Tarheels to win the Big Ten.

My skin had crawled at the silence in the park, but I had ignored it to focus on the problem of Julie. I was trying to figure out whether I loved her or just didn't want things to change.

Now I would never know.

Day broke, slowly.

Eventually, a figure approached my cell. A man about six and a half feet tall, heavyset, old, with a jowly face and the build of a man who had once been powerfully strong, now sagging muscles and wrinkled flesh. His eyes were a vivid violet, and they fixed me with a cold, disinterested gaze.

He touched a button and the color of the wall shifted slightly. He reached through the material, grabbed the food and water bowls, replaced them, touched the button once more. The whole process took less than thirty seconds, and it wasn't until he had finished that I realized I could have gone through the deactivated wall and escaped.

He turned on a heel and walked away, whistling a cheery tune, one hand resting on the handle of a gun holstered at his hip.

Perhaps staying in the cell had been the better choice after all.

I paced the cell, tried sleeping and failed, fell back to pacing restlessly, anger building.

Finally, I heard voices approaching, children laughing and squealing, parents scolding. I understood the tones of voice and rhythm and volume, but the words were unintelligible. A child stopped in front of me. He pointed at me, jabbered excitedly, leaned forward and spoke slowly, each word enunciated; he was reading, I realized. He met my eyes for a long moment, as if hypnotized.

"What do you want?" I asked.

The boy stumbled backward, his face crumpling into tears. He turned and ran, buried his face in his mother's belly, looked up at her, pointing at me. The boy's father approached my enclosure, read the words.

The father peered at me, squinting his eyes and leaning forward. He reached a hand up, touched his jawbone where it met the bottom of his ear; there was a soft electronic *beep*. *"Hallo? Verstehst du mich?"* he said. I just stared at him, shook my head. He touched his jaw again. "Hello? How about now?" English, with a bit of a British twang.

"Where the hell am I?" I demanded.

He laughed, as if the answer was obvious. "Why, you're in the zoo! This is the Megapolis City Zoo, don't you know. You're the newest exhibit: Old Earth Male."

It was at this moment, as I stumbled backward and fell against the cot, swearing and choking back a sob, that the second sun rose, huge and red, bathing the world an alien crimson.

As I Dream

come with me and I'll show you the world
walk with me, laugh with me, cry with me
press closer to me
let's dance, my love
show me your soul and I'll show you the stars
I'll clasp you to my breast
and listen to you breathe
come with me and we'll waltz through life
huddling beneath the weight of storms
gasping for breath
when the waves crash around us
come with me
explore the farthest reaches of desire
press closer to me
let's dance, my love

Be Now Porcelain

I am flying with wings
hidden and limber and shimmering
glittering in the brilliance of a noonday sun
I am laughing in cynical silence
cackling in mirth
speaking about your yesteryear actions
so heartless and cruel
and remembered nevermore
I am far beyond the quaking in fear
of your unwitting sins
against my heart and soul and world
I am wandering around
my rusting rotting inner temple
weeping for your love of me
once so tender and divine and fierce
these words are confusingly full of thoughts
crashing and clanging
banging and booming
full of calm and messy ideas
spoken and whispered
addressed to one whom I love
with the power of hurricanes and earthquakes and thunder
addressed to one who is futurely delicate
yet strong and complex and alluring

addressed to one whom I long to hold
now and yesterday and tomorrow
whose soft and salty skin I pray to press against
whom I dream of cradling close
bathed in the flickerlight of candles
with whom I long to talk
the whole star-flecked night through
next to whom I long to wake
in the flaming pink of sunrise
All these picturepainting words have been addressed
to a future one
with whom I plead
to whom I whisper questions
such as
who are you
where are you
why are you so long gone
so far distant
when will you become to me
flesh and blood and bone
rather than these dulcet fragments of dreaming
be not so untouchably angelic
be now porcelain to me
Sing to me an answer Angel
be not silent

Emerging Elegies: Haunting Refrains

Look at me, glance at me,
deign to meet my gaze;
in the deepest hours of this endless night,
when all is still, when even bright Luna
veils her solemn eyes
behind shreds and shrouds
of furling clouds,
when my roving restless mind
finds solace elusive and mercurial
in those times of darkest silence,
I wish for you.

But I am met with echoing ghosting memories
of nights past,
of hours passed
smoking and writhing together,
whispering and touching;
I am met with silence,
with vignettes of you,
scraps of you,
haunting refrains of you,
tangles of you caught in the sheets of our bed,
images of you, shadows of you
writhing on the walls,
scents of you lingering in the absence of you.

My eternal silence deepens further,
down to a vanishing point
of dissipating thoughts,
coruscating wishes,
ephemeral ideas.

Past all this,
from somewhere far and shadowed
I hear your siren song
drifting on desert winds,
pulsing with subsumed fervor.
When I hear your song, my distant siren,
in that stillest hour my silence breaks,
shatters.
What emerges then is an elegy,
the knelling cry of a soul bared
to a sleeping, heedless world.

My song is ringing in the ether,
do you hear it?
Though the music is strange,
straining up from my innermost reaches of self,
roiling voiceward
from out of my turbulent sea of desire,
can you hear it?

Can you feel the longing traced in these lines?
If you listen, you'll hear me, my siren.
You'll hear my keening canto

drifting on jungle winds,
shaking with deposed passion.
You'll hear me, my siren,
if only you'll listen.

Jack & Djinn

The night Moira died was a wild one, filled with awful, magical wonder.

She was a fey, beautiful slip of a thing, alive with mystery and love and passion and talent. Dark hair, of course, black as night, black as raven's wing, long and always loose except for the bangs tied back. Eyes like liquid jade, always-warm skin tanned from days spent reading in the sun, sketching on piers, swimming at the beach and running with her iPod…oh, she always had that iPod, she'd slip it from her pocket in odd moments, plug one bud into an ear, click up the volume and bob her head slightly, but she'd never miss a word of what was said around her. She sang in the shower, hummed when she sketched.

She always wore bright colors. She said that this mortal life was too short and too beautiful to dress drably.

She believed in magic and she drank scotch.

It started with a wedding. Her best friend Marie was getting married in Montauk; Moira was the maid of honor, and we were supposed to be there all weekend. We drove down on a Friday morning, shoving a few changes of clothes and some toiletries in her little brown suitcase, a battered thing covered with stickers of her favorite bands and lyrics written in Sharpie, and taped-on postcards from friends in exotic places. She knew so many people, had friends all over the world. I never knew how she accumulated so many friends, such eclectic people that always sent her a postcard. I guess I do know, though. She was always friendly, always willing to chat up a perfect stranger, could entrance you with her passionate, nonstop patter, could make you miss your train because you just forgot all about life when you were talking to her.

We drove to Montauk slowly, taking scenic routes and stopping to take pictures of benches and cute couples and interesting buildings. We stopped for lunch at a tiny little diner, drank hours-old coffee and ate corned beef Reubens. She laughed at my bad jokes, like she always did, and kissed me with brief passion as I held the door for her. She loved it when I held doors for her, so I did, because I liked making her happy, and because she always kissed me before she got in.

Montauk was lovely, of course. Marie and her fiancé Jared lived in a marvelous cottage by the sea, an old pale blue house with low eaves and white shutters and bamboo floors and a balcony that went all the way around the house.

"I love their house," Moira told me as we pulled up, parked the rusted red Honda with a *crunch* of gravel. "It's the kind of place where magic happens. You always feel at home here, even if you've never been. You can sleep without dreaming, and the coffee always tastes better. Even Folgers." I just laughed and grabbed the suitcase from the back seat. She waited for me to open the door for her, pecked me on the corner of the mouth, whispered in my ear, "the rooms have thick walls, and making love lasts forever."

I frowned. I hated thinking of her as having had other lovers, even though I knew she had, as had I. She was mine, and there never had been anyone else.

She must have read my mind, because she twined her fingers in mine, and looked at me. "That's what Marie tells me, at least. I've only ever been here alone. Cross my heart."

Cross my heart. She never said, "I promise." Only, "cross my heart." There was magic in the actual words, she always claimed. If you said it, you were bound to make it true, and if you didn't, something bad would happen. You could give your word just as well without binding yourself. It was only prudent.

She threw salt over her shoulder, never walked under ladders or stepped on cracks, or broke mirrors, or picked up face-down coins, or spoke ill of the dead. She always prayed before bed, because you never knew what could happen, and she said the Hail Mary at least once a day, even though she wasn't catholic, just because she loved the poetry in the words.

Marie was short, buxom, auburn-haired with green eyes. Moira said that she and Marie were bound together by their green eyes and the letter M. Jared was tall and muscular and tough-looking, with a hardness to his eyes that spoke of his tour in Afghanistan. The hardness never softened, except when he looked at Marie. They were one of those couples that seemed so opposite of each other, but somehow you just couldn't imagine them with anyone else.

They welcomed us into their home, set our suitcase on the third step from the bottom, poured us drinks, asked about our drive. They cooked us dinner—pulled pork sandwiches and homemade fries, salad with cherries and walnuts, homemade pecan pie with Cool Whip. Marie was a fantastic cook. Moira? Not so much. She could make a chicken pot pie that was to die for, but anything else was inedible. She used too much seasoning, I think, and I could never get her to measure. She said she'd grown up with the pinch and the dash, never the teaspoon or tablespoon.

The rest of the wedding party arrived around six, three more couples that neither Moira nor I really knew, and then later dozens of other guests. The party wound up quickly, with big band on the stereo and the drinks flowing in plenty, tiki torches lining the path to the beach where there was a massive, ten foot tall bonfire in the firepit and the scintillant glint of the moonlit sea.

At some point Moira had changed into a green dress, an elegant, unusual gown that she had made herself, I suspected; it clung to her slim, athletic body, cut low with long, pointed sleeves and flowers sewn on in random places, bright, handmade silk daisies of all colors. It seemed something more fit for a costume in

A Midsummer Night's Dream. It suited her perfectly, and drew my eyes to her wherever she was, dancing a two-step stomp around the fire with Marie and other girls, red plastic cups of wine in one hand, tambourines in the other, someone playing a guitar across the fire, someone talented, strumming and picking a lively, skirling flamenco tune, and then there was a fiddle and a tom-tom and the music was boiling in all our blood, picking us up and setting us in motion, almost against our will, as if the night and the music had conspired to enchant us. Moira was singing, suddenly, standing alone with her hands folded across her stomach, eyes closed, head tilted to one side, holding us captive with some song none of us knew in a strange and lilting tongue.

Then there was a man beside her, tall, hard-angled features, deep brown eyes and carefully trimmed beard, singing with her, putting a massive paw on her back with a familiarity that set my jealousy rising. She felt his touch, pulled away with a start and a look of fear in her eyes. He smiled at her, a curl of the lips that did not reach his eyes, pulled his hand away. He glanced at me, smirked, looked away.

Later, I found Moira alone, almost half a mile down the beach, bare feet in the surf, strolling slowly and gazing out to sea. I could sense her pensive mood, took my place alongside her without speaking immediately. I took her hand, watched the silver disk of the full moon shimmering distortedly on the surface of the sea, wavering as if turned to liquid itself, listened to the soft sensuous susurrus of the surf smashing against the shore.

At length, she spoke, slowly, choosing her words with deliberate care. "I know you don't like to think of my past, Jack. I've tried to respect that. But I think you deserve an explanation." She looked up at me, jade eyes limpid and hesitant. I squeezed her hand, nodded, tried to clear my head of preconceptions.

"That man," she continued, "is someone I knew a long time ago. His name is Caleb. We were together for…a long time." She turned her gaze to the sand at her feet, twisted a strand of hair. "We almost married, actually. Like, I ran away at the altar. I haven't seen him since, to be honest, and I always worried he'd just show up like this."

I tried to formulate a question that encompassed everything I was feeling. "So…should I be worried?" I felt a knot of fear coiled in my gut, a sense of my own past returning to haunt me. The last girl I had thought I loved had left me for an ex-boyfriend. I had a ring in my pocket when she told me. The girl before that I had caught in bed with my brother.

So, you could say I had trust issues.

"Well…yes, but not like you think. I left him because I realized I didn't love him, and I don't. I'm not leaving you or anything. I love you, Jack, it's just…he's a difficult person. He was really hurt when I left him like I did, and he's angry. Rightfully so. Now…I'm worried that he'll do something crazy. He's...a little weird. Unbalanced. Which is part of why I left him."

"Are you afraid of him?"

"Honestly, yes." She put a hand to her stomach, as if to soothe troubled nerves. "There's...a lot you don't know about me."

"Did he used to hurt you?" She just nodded. "Well then we have to make him leave. I'm sure Jared will make him, won't he?"

"Caleb is his brother."

"That complicates things."

"Just stay with me, Jack. I'm sure things will work out okay. Just...just don't leave me alone. Promise?"

I'd never seen her like that before. She never seemed afraid of anything. Even when facing difficulties, she kept her composure, seemed to be able to hold on to some core of buoyancy and joy. It was much of what made her so wonderful to be around, because her energy was contagious. Now, however, she seemed to be just sapped, drained by fear.

"Can't we just...leave?"

"No, Jack. I wish it was that easy. Marie is my best friend. We've known each other since we were five. And I'm her maid of honor."

I sighed. "I know. I know. I just don't know how to handle this."

"Some things you can't push down or run away from, or ignore and hope it goes away. I owe him an explanation, at least."

I just nodded. I felt a twinge of shame at her words. She knew me too well, knew that it was my tendency to do just that, run away from problems, or ignore them and hope for the best. She was braver than I, by far.

Caleb and Jared were sitting side by side, on a log near the fire. People had let the fire die down and gone back inside, away from the late night chill. The two men looked remarkably similar, now that I saw them together. Both absurdly good-looking, tall and muscular and lithe, both moved with a kind of pantherish grace that I envied. I was the type to trip over my own feet walking down the street. These men were athletic and confident, whereas I was bookish and introverted, more comfortable with my graphic novels and my cello than on the football field. Jared nodded at me, saluted me with his Coors bottle. Caleb just looked at me, not quite glaring, just regarding, assessing. He returned his attention to his brother after a moment, and I felt somehow dismissed, categorized as a non-threat. He picked up a discarded beer can from the sand by his feet, glanced at me sideways to make sure I was watching. Somehow, the can seemed to fit into the palm of his hand, an impossible distortion of proportions that wasn't dismissed by blinking or shaking my head. With another glance at me, this time with that same arrogant smirk, he crushed the can, squeezed hard enough to make his fist tremble. For a moment I would have sworn I saw his hand glow slightly, but then it was gone and I doubted myself. Caleb opened his hand, tossed the can to me with a flick. I fumbled, caught it; the can had been crushed into a ball the size of a large marble. It was still hot—so hot I had to juggle it and toss it into the sand at my feet.

Caleb just winked at me, like an uncle who has pulled a quarter from his nephew's ear.

Moira had wandered to the house by herself, despite her own plea to not be left alone. I could just see her on the deck with a glass in her hand, talking to Marie, gesturing animatedly, Marie trying to calm her. I pocketed the ball of aluminum and crunched through the sand back up to the house, found a bottle of beer and joined Marie and Moira.

"He swears he's changed," Marie was saying, her voice low but insistent. "He just wants to talk. Give him five minutes, please. You're my best friend and he's about to be my brother-in-law. I want you to get along. Please." Marie glanced at me, gave me a small polite smile of acknowledgment. I stood next to Moira, my hand on her waist. She pushed against me, shoulder to my ribs. I wanted Caleb to see us. I wanted to show possession, if only in a passive-aggressive way.

"I don't know what there is to talk about. I'll apologize for I how I left, but that's it. He's apologized for what he did to me, dozens of times. It doesn't make a difference."

"It does to him. Just give him a chance, Moira."

"A chance for what? Reconciliation? Even if I

wasn't with Jack, I wouldn't go back to Caleb. I don't care how much he's changed."

Marie shook her head and sighed, drank from her glass. "You're not being reasonable."

"Reasonable?" Moira was suddenly angry. "Reasonable? Why should I be *reasonable*, Marie? You know what he was like. You know what he did. Do you remember that night a week before the wedding, when I showed up at your apartment? Do you?"

Marie nodded, quiet suddenly, eyes conflicted. The things they were saying was raising a host of questions in my head, and I couldn't find my voice to speak them.

"Of course I remember," Marie whispered. "I hated him, that night. Even Jared was angry. I couldn't believe he would do…that." Without specifics, all I could do was guess, but I got the gist of it. Caleb had beaten her badly one night, obviously. And now he wanted to talk. I glanced at the fire, at the two figures still talking. I could feel Caleb's gaze on me like an itch under the skin.

"I'll talk to him," Moira said, "but not alone. If he has anything to say, he can say it in front of you and Jared and Jack."

"He won't like that."

"I don't *care* what he likes. It's that or nothing."

Marie nodded, descended the faded gray wooden steps to the beach, sat down next to Jared. I turned to Moira, showed her the ball of aluminum that had been the beer can. She cursed, took it in her hand and rolled it around her palm.

"Figures he would do that. He obviously hasn't changed that much. He's just trying to intimidate you."

"Well, it's working." There was so much I wanted to say, but I didn't know where to start. "What did he do to you, Moira? Honestly."

"Honestly?" She drained her glass, poured more scotch from a bottle sitting on the railing. She was a little tipsy, I realized. She rarely drank enough to get even tipsy, claiming she got enough high from life that she didn't need drugs or alcohol. I had believed her, but now I suspected there was more to it. She slugged back the amber liquid angrily, ice clinking and clattering, an almost masculine motion that made me uncomfortable, somehow. I could feel the emotions coming off of her, intense waves of fear and anger. She seemed hard, suddenly, diamond-hard, rather than steel-hard. Beautiful and impenetrable.

"Honestly...he used to beat the shit out of me. The worst part was, he wasn't a drunk, he was just mean. Violent. He and Jared, they joined the corps together, served in the same unit, went through the same tour in Afghanistan. They both came home different, but Jared, he handled it better. He was able to adjust, saw a counselor, worked it out in his own head. He still has his moments, but he's okay, overall." Moira leaned against the railing, bottle in one hand, glass in the other, eyes glazed and staring at Caleb. She was next to me, but a world away. "Caleb didn't deal quite as well with the things he experienced over there. He'd drink, and that would loosen him up, and it definitely didn't help, but he wasn't the typical alcoholic wife-beater you think of.

"Well, that night, a week before we were supposed to get married, he came home from the bar, late. I'd stayed up to finish a painting. I should have gone to bed, and I knew it, because it was always worse if I was awake when he got home late. Well, I stayed up, finished the painting, and he came in roaring drunk. The one time he'd been that wasted in all the time I'd known him. Apparently he and Jared had run into some buddies from the service and they'd had a grand old time telling war stories. He knocked me around pretty bad. Broke a couple ribs, and my nose. I finally ran, went to Marie's. I swore that night that I'd never go back to him, but of course he found me, and charmed me back.

"That's the story. I was coming down the aisle, wearing his ten thousand dollar ring and Vera Wang dress, and I saw him waiting for me. It was a little thing that did it. He flexed his hand—you know, out of nerves, clenched his fist and let it go, wiped his palm on his pants leg. But that split-second, when he clenched his fist…I had this vision of being thirty, forty years old, having his kids, bringing his beer, him bouncing me off the walls…I was about to become my mom, and…and I just—I couldn't do it.

"I dropped the bouquet on the floor, pulled off the ring and set it on the arm of the pew. I ran, kicked off my heels, and ripped out the veil. I took a cab to Aunt

Helena's house in Atlantic City. I stayed in her extra bedroom with the porcelain dolls and 'Nsync posters for a week straight. Eventually I moved to Manhattan and met you, and tried not think about him ever again."

I suspected that she had left out a bit in between moving to Manhattan and meeting me, but I let it go. I could tell how hard it had been to talk about that, and she was downing the scotch like it could burn away the memories.

"Moira…" I rolled the marble of aluminum in my fingers, glanced at her, watched her shift uncomfortably, take a long swig to hide her thoughts from me. "How did he do this? I swear I saw his fist glow, and even without that, he shouldn't be able to do this. This was a beer can. I don't care how strong he is, this isn't normal."

"Oh, Jack. Can't you just let it go? Just…chalk it up to something weird?"

"Why should I have to? The fact that you're being so blatantly evasive tells me it's not nothing."

"What if I told you that you *really* don't want to know? Jack, baby, listen." Her eyes were burning, intense, glittering with refracted moon-glaze and starshine. "There are things that you don't know about me. I've told you this already. Some of them aren't easy-to-explain things, like an abusive ex. This is one of them. Please, just let it go. Please? For me? I really want to just get through this wedding and have things go back to normal."

"And if you told me…whatever it is you don't want to tell me…then we couldn't go back to normal?"

"Basically, yes."

I sighed. "I'll try." I knew I couldn't pretend, though, and so did she. We both knew that this would eat away at me. It would have been easier if she'd just acted like she didn't know what I was talking about, but she's a terrible liar.

Curiosity killed the cat, they say.

Things slowed down, and eventually people found couches and beds to crash on, and by 3 a.m. there was only the six of us awake. That's when the real weirdness began.

We all ended up at the firepit, nursing drinks and feeling the world spin beneath us too fast, too wobbly. The sand was cold under our bare feet, the sky wide and black and washed with stars. Fire crackled, spat, popped, and the sea whispered secrets to us in her old slow language of waves lapping and crashing.

The silence was awkward, and difficult. Marie tried to make small talk, but Jared seemed lost in thought, and the tension between Caleb, Moira and I was thick and palpable.

"Okay, you know what? This is stupid." Marie shot to her feet, a bit unsteadily, and turned her gaze on each of us in turn. "It's two days before my wedding, and none of the people I love the most can get along." We all held our silence. I dug a hole in the sand by my feet with a stick, and Caleb swirled the dregs of his beer slowly; Moira sat beside me, clicking a Zippo open and closed. Jared just stared at the stars.

"Caleb," Marie pleaded, "if you have something to say, then just say it. This is the only chance you'll ever have. I promise you."

Caleb snorted, shuffled his feet, dug his toes under the sand. "Not bloody likely, Marie. Not in front of *him*." The last word was spat, as if it left a bad taste in his mouth. He reached behind him into a blue-lidded cooler, popped open another beer.

"He's not so bad, Cay. And he loves Moira."

"You say that like it's supposed to help. He's a *tyro*, Marie."

What the hell was a tyro? I opened my mouth to ask, but Moira elbowed me, shook her head slightly. I took a drink instead.

"I know," Marie answered, "but he takes better care of her than—" She cut herself off short.

"Than I ever did? Don't remind me. I hate how I was. I regret it every single day." Caleb chugged his beer as if it could erase the past, finished it, clenched a massive fist around the neck of the brown glass bottle, stared hard at it, squeezed. There was a soft *pop* and the glass exploded in his hand; instead of shards of glass and blood, sand fell from his fingers and blew away in the wind. He flexed his hand, darted a glance at me, and then addressed Moira.

"Listen, Moira," he began, "I know I was an asshole to you. I know that sorry can't even begin to cover it. I wish it could. If there was some way to make it up to you, or go back and undo it, or redo it, I would. But not even I can turn back time. I know this doesn't count for much, but...forgive me, Moira. You deserved better than me."

Moira pinched the bridge of her nose, sighed through clenched teeth. She looked up at him, and I did not envy Caleb the glare she leveled at him.

"No, it doesn't count for much. It doesn't count for anything at all. You weren't just an asshole, Caleb. You *beat* me. An asshole forgets anniversaries, goes to the titty bar with his buddies on the weekends or...I don't even know what. You were supposed to *be there* for me! Not hit me. Not break four of my ribs. You...you were supposed to *love* me, goddamn you! I gave you six years of my life, and all I got in return were bruises and broken bones. And I *hate* you for bringing all this back up. For making me cry like this in front of Jack."

She turned to me. Her eyes were no longer green, they were orbs of flame, literal suns writ miniature, her skin was bronze and glowing redly and radiating heat so fierce that I had to shift away.

"Jack...Jack...I'm sorry. I never wanted you to see me like this. I love you, I do. With all my heart, I love you. I love you like I've never loved anyone, in ten thousand years I've never loved anyone like you."

She was all aflame now, her hair wafting upwards like a bonfire, her skin burnished metal hissing with heat and shifting like molten steel. She reached a hand to touch me, a crackling finger extended to brush my face as she so often did, stopped herself before she set me alight; she sobbed, a wrenching cry of sorrow that cracked my soul like a dropped mirror.

I couldn't function. I couldn't breathe the superheated air around Moira, couldn't breathe for the shattered pieces of my heart, couldn't speak or curse or even shake my head to express the shock. Why was I so brokenhearted? My thoughts, my emotions were swirling around the vortex of a single question: what *was* she? I knew *who* she was, and I sensed she still was that person, but she was someone—some*thing* else, as well. I tried to ask myself if I could love her despite this, for this, because of this…no answer came. I couldn't formulate the question, couldn't consider the answer. I could only stare at her awful, beautiful, hypnotic form, the same slim, feminine curves, the same sway of hip, the same delicate bird-frail shoulders, the same lips I loved to kiss, the same Moira, only carved in living flame, untouchable. She turned her eyes to me, and I could feel the brush of love in them, despite the fiery alien ferocity of them.

"Can you still love me, Jack?" Her voice was different, ethereal, tolling like a bell, musical and ringing and echoing. "Can you love me, like this?"

"What…what are you?"

"I am a jiniri. A djinn…a genie." She said the words as if she were pronouncing a curse on herself. As if she knew the answer. "No, of course you can't." She turned to Caleb, moved toward him. She didn't walk; she drifted, floated like a spark on a breeze.

"You." Now her voice was quiet, calm, and deadly. "I do *not* forgive you. I cannot. Will not." She lifted a hand, palm out, as if gesturing *stop*. A gout of flame leapt from her palm like a striking serpent and hit Caleb full on the chest, enveloped him, ignited him. He didn't scream, didn't flail or drop to the ground. He simply absorbed the flames, fed from them to grow larger still, skin hardening and cracking and turning to chunks of stone; the flames extinguished, and Caleb stood a dozen feet high, no longer a man but a creature of granite and magma with glowing-coal eyes. The two stood facing each other, unmoving, unspeaking, a frozen tableau, Jared impassive to one side, Marie shaking her head in denial.

Caleb lifted a fist, suddenly somehow four-fingered and boulder-sized and afire, larger than my head; he swung at Moira, a slow and powerful swipe that impacted with a *whoompf* and an explosion of flame and rock shards that lit into my skin, carving runnels of blood and blistering skin. I felt a solid mass crash into my side and knock me to the sand, patting out flickering spurts of fire on my clothes and hair. My savior, Jared, was muttering under his breath in a guttural, rasping language that sounded like shifting shale and cracking stones.

"You don't wanna get caught in the middle of this, human boy," Jared said, speaking with a harsh accent.

He'd always spoken precisely, in the clear, educated manner of someone who had worked hard to overcome an accent, or to hide it. "This gonna be rough one, these two had this fight comin' for years, and it not gonna stop till one of them or the other is dead. You best run far away, Jack-boy, and don't look back, just forget about Moira. It be best for you, I think."

He lifted me up by the arm, jerking me off the ground as if I were a toddler. He positioned his body between me and Moira and Caleb, who were striking each other furiously, each blow spattering gobbets of liquid flame and bits of rock. A shove to the back sent me flying, rolling over and over in the sand, sliding to a stop just at the water's edge, licked by frigid seawater. I could hear the blows connected, a grunt of pain, a shriek of rage, a roar of billowing flame that seared me even from a dozen feet away. I could only see the stars and the sea and the moon, and it seemed peaceful, oblivious to the horror behind me. I couldn't move, only lay shocked and numb. Then the earth shook next to me and I rolled over enough to see Caleb standing above me, fire dripping from a fist like the blood of a sun, the same strange gore splattered on his face, his chest, sizzling and vanishing. He fell to his knees, crushing my outflung hand beneath him, stared down at me with eyes expressing emotions I couldn't interpret, something like confusion, pain, sorrow, loss. He collapsed face-down and the heat from his body crisped and curled the hair on my head, my three-day growth of beard; the heat began to dissipate and the bright orange magma peeking out from between the cracks of his skin cooled and dulled and dimmed, the banked fire of his eyes faded and then, abruptly, he was no longer man nor granite giant, but a pile of boulders in the sand, rocks shifting and settling.

I struggled to an elbow, then to my hands and knees, thinking that I should feel some kind of emotion at what was obviously death. I lurched to my feet, feeling dread in my gut like lead.

She lay half in the firepit, the flames of her body merging with the bonfire. I tried to run over to her, succeeded only in falling face-first in the sand, rose back up spitting grit, a sob caught in my throat.

I knew the answer, as I saw Moira lying prone and vulnerable and dying. I knew that I would love her no matter what she may have been. I realized I had been half hoping that this would be a drunken dream, that I would wake up in bed with sun streaming in through the window, Moira spooned against my stomach. I knelt down next to her, knowing by the agony of fire against skin that I was awake, caught up in something I couldn't understand. *There's a lot you don't know about me,* she had said. What an understatement that was. I didn't know anything about her, not even the Moira that I thought was a normal, if eccentric, human girl with a mysterious past and mile-high walls around her heart. I didn't know about her dead parents, or that she had had brother, or how they died. And now she was a genie, a...a djinn she had said, a jiniri, and did such mythical beings even *have* parents and brothers? Were they djinni as well? What was Caleb? Jared? Marie? If Caleb and Moira had had child, what would it have been? If Moira and I had?

The questions rocketed through my skull, banging and burning and echoing and repeating, all without answer.

She looked at me, and her eyes shifted briefly to the familiar green pools I loved so well, and her voice, when she spoke, was the lyrical lilt of the girl Moira, not the knelling bell of a djinn.

"Do you love me, Jack?" She was pleading, desperate; she was mournful, as if she knew the answer.

I tried to speak, could only nod, choke on my words. Was she dying? Could djinn die? I drew breath, forced the words out, precise and careful: "I love you, Moira. I love you."

I had never said the words before. My own walls had always prevented me, before. It had been a sore point, before, because I couldn't say it. I did all I could to show her, to make her know it, but to actually say the words, out loud, to her...it was too hard. Too many old, scabbed-over wounds split open if I tried.

Moira half laughed, half sobbed. "Even like this?" She lifted a hand in front of her face, watched it burn.

"Yes, even like this. You're still you, aren't you? Even if you are...some kind of mythical creature." I wanted to touch her, to comfort her, couldn't.

Moira struggled to a sitting position, each movement eliciting a subdued whimper. She was so close now that my skin was tightening from the heat. "Trust me," she said, so softly that I almost didn't hear it.

Before I could respond, she leaned forward and kissed me, plunged a hand through my chest. A sudden burst of pain was all I felt, rather than the awful agony I expected. I thought I would be immolated, but somehow, I wasn't. I was burning, but not consumed, not destroyed. I felt something spark within me, combust and blaze into furious life. I felt Moira in my very soul, felt her presence in my mind, her essence in my heart, her heat in my body. It was orgasmic, but not sexual, a consummation of love, an expression of unity that no mere physical act could rival. For a moment, I was flame, and she was flesh; I was eternal, and she was mortal.

Time stuttered, froze. Moira pulled away, and for brief moment, I saw her as one entity, a living woman and an undying jiniri, two identities, two forms, forever tangled. She was never more lovely than in that moment; I knew, then, that for as long as I lived I would never, ever forget that moment, when I saw her as she really was, fully flesh and fully fire.

There was a sound as of a million voices singing in harmony, a choir of sorrow and peace in elegant juxtaposition; when the voices fell silent, all at once, Moira was gone. There was a sudden wind, a long, howling, heaven-shuddering coriolis wind that culled all of the heat from the world in one gust, and she was no more. No body to bury, no keepsake to mourn over, just the memory of her skin against mine, her lips against mine, her laughter and her weird, lovable, lovely ways.

"Goodbye, Moira." I whispered the words to still air, to the silver sea singing in susurrus, to the moon that had watched this all occur.

There is no time in the spaces between realms, between heaven and earth, between the dens of angels and the caverns of demons. There is no time, because there is no finite mortal being to segment the passage of time into seconds and minutes, centuries and millennia.

The spirit that floated in this timeless wasteland was female. It knew it was female, but had no thoughts of self, or occurrence or causality. She only knew sorrow, but not the why of her sorrow. She floated, and if she could have wept, she would have, loudly and without ceasing, but she had no body with which to weep.

The spirit was not precisely dead, for she was a djinn, and thus immortal. But when she died in her mortal body, she was returned to the realm from which she came. She had no knowledge of the passage of time, of course, so she could not know how long she dwelt there, in that homeworld of fire and magic, but she knew she was discontent. She could not remain. So she left, in search of that which she had lost, something of great value, but what it was, she did not know. So she searched the many realms, drifting as a spirit, incorporeal and invisible, watching and discerning.

Then she felt a twinge of pain, a brief knife of knowledge slicing into her as she passed through from one realm to another, from the space between to a place of physicality, of dirt and sky and water and fire and blood and love. She had known this place, once, the spirit realized. She had lived here, had trod the earth and breathed the air. The throbbing pain in her soul was the blade of memory. As she wafted between the sun and the clouds, she felt herself assaulted by memory after memory, striking her like hail. She saw, in all the memories, a man. His face caused emotions to roil within her, love, sorrow, desire, all tangled and twisted together; she knew it was this man that she had lost, him that was causing her such sorrow. Had he died? She could not remember what had happened, but she knew her sorrow was connected to him, somehow.

So, she searched for him. She moved through cities, apparent only in the rustle of a stray newspaper, the flutter of a flag, the clatter of a discarded can, the howl of the wind between buildings. Eventually, she found him.

He was not young, any longer. His brown hair was shot with gray, his skin sagged in places and he moved with a stiffness that spoke of age. But his eyes were the same, deep brown, like rich soil or polished cherrywood. His eyes held secrets, an aged, weathered sadness that had never healed. He had lived, and loved. There was a ring on his finger, a worn and faded gold band, and his mind contained memories of a kind woman with soft blond hair and delicate hands. She had loved him, this woman, thoroughly and truly, but she had always known of the secret sorrow in his soul, and she had always known there was a portion of him that could not love her completely. She had known, and she had accepted it, for he did love her, if imperfectly. There were children, three of them, now grown. There was a successful career, and a comfortable retirement on the horizon. But, as the spirit perused his memories and his heart, she knew he was becoming more and more restless. His wife knew it as well.

The spirit entered their home, the man and his wife's. She watched as they ate in silence, the man alone with his thoughts and the wife watching him, missing him, wondering where he was.

The spirit felt as if she had once loved this man, with a body as well as with the immortal essence of herself. She examined him, wondering if there were any clues within him to who she had been, when she had lived on this fleeting earth. She looked deep in his memories, and there, hidden away and hoarded carefully, she saw a vision of herself, slim and small-breasted, dark hair and green eyes. The spirit grasped at that memory, tried to pull it into herself, to become that woman of flesh and blood once again.

Her memory of life as a mortal being was hazy

and slippery, and thus she had no way of knowing how her sudden appearance would affect the man and his wife. All she knew was that she needed him, this man.

~

There was a sound like crashing cymbals, the air shuddered and wavered and split; a pyre of flame seared the air, trembled, resolved itself into the form of a woman, carved in liquid, living flame. Then, slowly, beginning at her hands and feet and the tips of her hair, the flames cooled and morphed into the skin of a mortal woman, naked, lovely, and serene.

Jack's heart thudded, stopped, stuttered, resumed beating. He felt tears on his face. He hadn't wept when he married Kara, or when his children were born, or when Kara had miscarried at thirty weeks. He hadn't wept since Moira died.

And now, without warning, after thirty years, here she was.

"Jack?" Her voice was as he remembered, the reverberating knell of a djinn. She sounded hesitant, unsure of herself. "Is that your name? I remember you, your form. I remember that I loved you…and that this body is how I appeared. Yes, your name is Jack. You loved to read books, your favorite musician was Benny Goodman. You spoke in your sleep, and you liked to talk after we made love."

Kara, beside him, made a sound that was somewhere between a laugh and a sob.

"Yes, Moira," Jack said. "It's me. Where did you go? How did you come back? I thought you died."

"I am a djinn. We cannot die, not truly. Our bodies, when we take this human form, can die, here on this earth of yours. But our essence, that which makes us djinni, that cannot die."

"Why did you come back, then?"

"I was discontent among the other djinn. I didn't know why, until I found you. Somehow, I need you. Djinni have often taken mortal lovers; your people have stories about this. I do not know how, but we are bound together. There is a part of my essence within you, and yours within me. From that day on the beach. I put part of myself within you. So I could always find you again."

Moira looked to Jack's wife, standing with a hand over her mouth, tears brimming but not falling. "I'm sorry. I did not mean to take him from you."

"You didn't take him from me," Kara said, voice shaky. "I have had twenty-five years with him. I've always known there was a part of him that wasn't mine." She looked from Jack to the djinn. "Or do you mean that you *are* taking him from me, now?"

"Yes," Moira said. "He is mine. I am sorry. I do not know any other way. I do not wish for you to be hurt."

Jack turned to his wife, took her in his arms. "I love you," he told her, whispered it in her ear. "You are my wife. She's my past." He turned to the djinn...to Moira, "I can't go with you. Maybe if you had come back long ago, I might have. Now? After twenty-five years? Just leave her? I'm sorry, but no."

Moira looked puzzled. "But...you must." Her eyes, green and luminous, seemed to flicker and blaze alight. "You *must*." She reached out, took Jack by the arm, pulled him to her with an inexorable, irresistible strength. "You must. You are mine."

She held him against her, and Jack struggled to resist the sensation of desire building within him at the feel of her skin, silk-smooth and radiating heat, young and firm and intoxicating. He looked to Kara, his wife, the woman with whom he'd spent his life, and he reached for her, even as he felt himself being drawn away.

"Go, Jack," Kara said. She didn't mean it, he could tell. She was trying to be brave, and he loved her the more for it.

The djinn wrapped him up in her arms, and Jack felt his body responding, felt his heart cracking open; the love he'd buried deep, pushed down and denied for so many years came welling up. He fought against it, tried to focus in on Kara, but the air around him was blurred and wavering, shimmering with heat and crackling with magic. He couldn't see her anymore, only a vague outline, and even that was fading. Moira's arms were locked around him, and her face was in front of his, her lips were pressed against him, tasting of flame and smoke.

She burst alight, and he was once again burning but unconsumed, and this time he gave into it, surrendered, ignored the loud, insistent voice that called him coward and traitor. It was silenced, then, subsumed by the flames and desire and remembered love; it was silenced, but not gone.

Kara, watching, saw her husband devoured by the woman, the genie. He was enveloped by her arms and the licking fire of her body, and then, with a soft breath and the scent of sulfur, they were gone, and she was alone.

Kara sat in the silence, the only sound her breathing and her heart beating, and a clock ticking away the seconds.

She sat, and the seconds turned into hours. There was sleep, fitful, tearful, restless, on the couch.

She woke to the sun shining in her eyes, heat baking her skin. She smelled smoke, sulfur.

She sat up, and the world was on fire. It was so hot she felt the edges of her hair crisping, curling. Felt her skin tightening, bronzing, aching. Her lungs struggled against the heat. She couldn't open her eyes all the way, couldn't look directly at the source of the flames.

"Kara."

His voice.

She knew his voice with the intimacy of a lifetime spent hearing him speak, yell, whisper, groan, mutter.

"Jack?" She struggled to rise, to reach for him, heedless of the pain.

Abruptly, the flames vanished, and there he was. Her Jack.

But not…him.

This was the Jack she'd first met. Youthful, energetic. This wasn't her Jack of twenty-five years. This was her Jack of one hour, one day, one month.

Yet, as he staggered naked toward her, hair smoking, his eyes were his. The warm brown sweet loving eyes she'd always known, and they looked at her with the love of twenty-five years. He knew her, with the intimacy of all those years.

He collapsed to his knees at her feet, clutched at her legs, and sobbed. Head pressed against her thighs, chest heaving, sobbing as he'd not sobbed in all the years she'd known him. "Kara, Kara."

She hesitantly threaded her fingers through his hair, and the feel of him was familiar.

Home; Jack.

"I'm here, Jack."

"She took me there. To her home." He was choking, gasping, lungs fire-singed, voice hoarse. "It was… like the old descriptions of Hell—fire, lakes of fire. Mountains of obsidian. The buildings were…thousands of feet tall, crafted out of…out of obsidian, but as if it had been melted into liquid and reshaped. There millions of them, like her, but no two alike." A silence. "It was…beautiful."

"Jack, I…" Kara had no clue what to say.

"Beautiful, and horrifying. And Moira, she…she was different. She'd lost herself, the part of herself that was human, that was…the Moira I knew." Another sob, this one quieter. "I begged her to take me back. But her magic was…it was too strong. Too much. It was inside me. She'd put it there the day she died. It was me—her magic was me, her fire was me. I don't—I don't know."

"Do…do the kids have it?"

He shook his head. "I…I don't know. I don't think so. It was in my soul, not my DNA. I don't know." He sat back on his heels, looked up at her.

His eyes, for a moment, glowed. His skin heated. Burned.

"She saw that I wasn't hers anymore."

"So she let you go? Sent you back?"

A shake of his head. "No. She wouldn't. *Couldn't.* The thing which bound us, her magic, it was…it was *her*. Part of her essence. She truly does need me. Did."

"Jack, what happened?"

"She cried. When her tears fell, they sounded like drumbeats." He closed his eyes, fought to breathe. "She grew. Ten feet tall. A hundred. A thousand. Grew and grew, until she was everything. All around me. There was…I don't want to say an explosion…more of an implosion. Compressing down into a ball the size of a softball, but with all the mass and heat and energy and magic of the her that had been a hundred thousand feet tall."

He stood up. He *was* glowing.

"What did she do to you, Jack?" Kara touched his chest, and her fingers sizzled on his skin.

"Went into me. Into my chest—into my soul. And…and…*became*."

"Became…what? Became you?"

A shake of his head. "No. She's—she has a soul, but it's…dispersed. Into an infinite number of atoms. All inside me." He swallowed hard. "I can feel the…the *otherness* of her, but it's not a her, anymore, it's…*it*. I don't know how to put it into words."

She wanted to be closer. "Jack, I…I don't understand."

"Me either."

She inched closer, wincing at the heat of him. "Now what?"

"I don't know that either."

"Can you make yourself not so…hot?" Kara asked.

He screwed up his face, concentrating, and suddenly he was…more like just Jack again. "Better?"

She touched his face, smoothing fingertips along wrinkle-free corners of eyes, mouth. "No fair. You're young again."

He laughed. "Young? Kara, I think I'm *immortal*."

"What about…" she swallowed, searching his eyes with her own fearful ones. "What about me?"

He met her eyes. "The last thing she said to me, before she…" he waved his hands, wiggled his fingers—"went into atoms, was that if I wanted to, I could trade my forever. Give it to you. I wouldn't be immortal anymore—I'd be giving it to you. You'd be like me, changed into…this. She'd be part of you. What that means, I don't know. What it will feel like, I don't know. I just know that she told me how to do it. That I had to choose. And that I'd be giving up forever, but getting another lifetime with you."

"Why didn't you stay with her, Jack? You loved her. I saw that. I always knew someone else had a piece of you I'd never have."

"You're my wife, Kara. I loved her, yes, but... she died. I moved on. Healed, as best I could. Fell in love with you." He cupped her cheeks, and his hands heated, but it wasn't painful, now. "We have children together. A grandchild on the way. A lifetime together. I had a couple years with her, and a lifetime with you."

"But, Jack—"

"I didn't know what she was until the day she died. I still don't know any more about what it is or how it's possible than you do. I just know that you're my wife. I said I do, and I said till death do us part. I meant that."

"She took you from me." Kara was crying.

"Yes."

"She kept that piece of you from me our whole lives."

"Yes."

"And now she's part of you."

"Yes."

"And you're immortal, and I'm old. I'll live another twenty years, thirty maybe? Get old, decrepit, and you'll be young forever."

"But, Kara—"

"And if I want to be young, to have you, to be with

you, my husband, I have to take that essence of *her*… into *me?*"

Jack sighed. "Yeah." He brushed at her tears with his thumb. "When you put it like that…"

She touched his lips. "I just have one more question, my love."

"Anything."

"Does she…*know?* Is she aware?"

Jack shook his head. "That was her sacrifice. She couldn't live without me. But she couldn't keep me. So, she did…this. Whatever it is. She's not a sentient being anymore. Just…a force. An energy. Best I can tell, at least."

Kara nodded. "Well, then."

She stepped back out of Jack's arms. Began removing her clothing.

"Kara?" Jack murmured. "What…what are you…?"

She folded her clothing neatly and set it on the couch. "Those are my favorite jeans and sweater. I don't want the fire to ruin them."

Jack smiled. "So…"

Kara took his hand. "So, I'm ready."

"You're sure?"

"Twenty-five years and three kids, Jack." She squeezed his hand. "Yes, I'm sure. I said I do, too. Till death do us part. The vows didn't cover *this,* exactly, but I said forever, and I meant it."

Jack wrapped her up in his arms, kissed her.

Heat billowed. Flames crackled, spread like

wildfire. She felt the heat in her bones. Felt it in her pores, her blood. Felt her blood boiling, but his kiss was more, was hotter, was the kiss of love which had conceived their children. She burned, but was not consumed.

A flare of light, blue-white-yellow-orange.

Heat, beyond heat. Beyond fire—the sun itself burning within her.

Heat, then…

Liquid fire in her veins, pulsing between her synapses. Pounding in her skull, in her soul.

Fire, everywhere, everything.

Kara opened her eyes, and saw the pillar of fire, man-shaped, that was Jack, her husband. Her everything.

Just Jack.

Author's note: This short story was the genesis for what later became a novel of the same name. We always liked this story, and we're excited to share it with you here.

REFRACTIONS: HAIKU

magic in your eyes
ghostly presence of your touch
these I memorize

rain like daggers falls
slicing shadows and our words
we drown in silence

memory:
your hips against mine
afterglow

this silence profound
shaping our thoughts, unspoken
catalyzing touch

streetlights change
endlessly cycling through
green amber and red

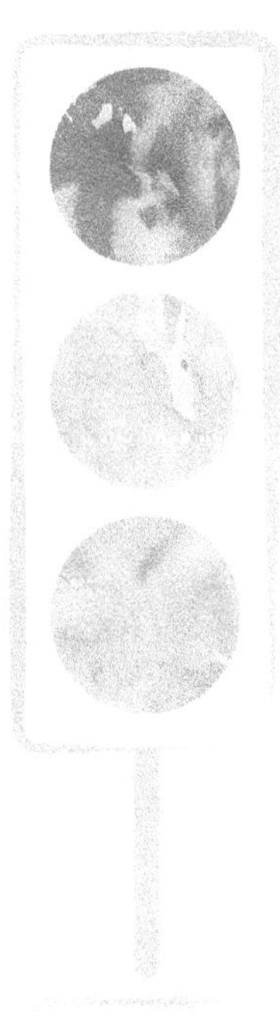

rain falls, a downpour
a ghosting silver torrent
umbrellas blooming

days and eons pass
quicker than thought, or eyeblink
a flickframe montage

deep into night
aching for your warmth
where are you?

sweat, scratches
lie back, exhausted
contented

empty streets
lights pull me onward
wanderlust

steaming tea
fractions of silence
pen rustles

blurry world
dizzy, unstable
drank too much

sun through falling rain
river of silver pearls
a morphing curtain

REFLECTIONS:
Untitled Poems

your eyes
and the curve of your hips
your smile
and your midnight whispers
candlelight on your skin

the wild soft wet warmth
of your kiss
your hands sliding over my back
fingernails on my shoulders
heels against my thighs

the shine of your eyes, wild
the bell of your laughter, ringing
the sweep of your hair by candlelight, alluring
rolling over to nuzzle you at 3 a.m., sweetly
the strength in your soul
and the gentility in your heart,
you

god I love you so damn much
I think
it's hard to be sure sometimes
because
love is an action
and I'm just so fucking selfish

generosity
is an art form
I fumble with brushes
while you, my love,
are Mattisse
Klimt
van Gogh

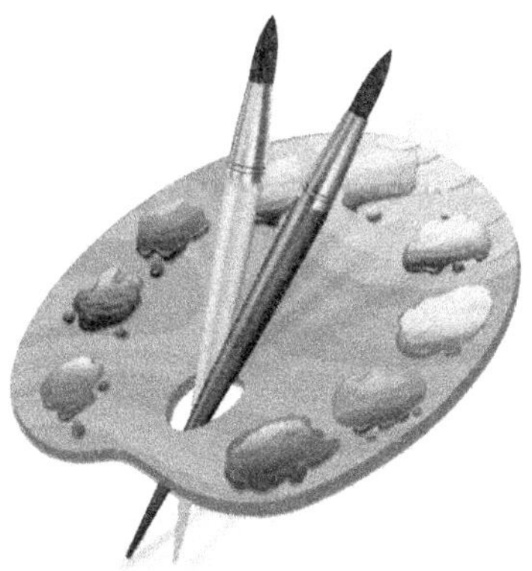

romance me, you say
like in the books we write
make me feel adored, treasured
meanwhile, I'm still standing here
blinded and dazzled
wondering, ten years in,
why you still love me

it's on the tip of my tongue
the pads of my fingers
whispering in ghostly skirls across the keyboard
in the ink of my pen
the saliva on my tongue
how to describe, truly
what my love for you is like

you roll over in your sleep
nudge me so I will roll with you
nuzzle your nose between my shoulder blades
murmur a small wordless sound of contentment
I love you so fiercely in those moments
that it's hard to breathe

your hand in mine
your hips swaying to the beat
you smile at me as if I hung the moon
I'm off-rhythm because your beauty
leaves me off-kilter
—dancing in the candlelight

if I could see angels
hear them sing
shudder at their presence
burn up in the fire of all their glory
still it would not rival the vision of you,
sleepy,
at dawn

to have and to hold
in sickness and in health
for richer or for poorer
till death do us part

we've tested them all, except the last one

sometimes apropos of seemingly nothing
your claws come out, razor-sharp
your walls slam into place, a mile high
your spikes slice out, like lances
but then you smile or laugh, and the sun returns

your sorrow is bitter
your resentment vicious
your depression brutal
your panic visceral
one laugh, one smile
and it's all erased

Sadness and hurt
Fear and fury
Even these are beautiful on you
They humanize your otherwise perfection

your breath whispers silver
nose nuzzling my neck
fingers dancing cold against my nape
laughter in my ear sweet and musical
—kissing in the winter

Before the Rooster Crows

It's a moment I'll never forget. How could I? It was the defining moment of my life, an instant imprinted indelibly on the fabric of my soul. If I close my eyes, even now, a lifetime later, sitting with aching joints waiting for guards to come and carry me to my own cross, I can see it all unfold:

Torchlight flickers, the hobnailed boots of the soldiers echo as they tramp through Caiaphas' house…I follow Him at a distance, unwilling or unable to accept what is happening. He foretold it, I know, but seeing it happen… it's unreal. My heart is beating like a Roman galley drum, my throat is tight with fear, I am breathless; if they know I am one of His followers, they might take me too, do to me what they are doing to Him…my flesh shivers at the thought of the scourge tips ripping my flesh. I cannot bear that thought, but neither can I leave Him. So I follow, hoping they don't ask too many questions.

It was only three years or so, but they changed me completely. I was a fisherman, simple, strong, and stubborn. I took my boat out in the early morning, when dawn's fingers were just brushing the horizon, threw my net and hauled it in, again and again until my muscles ached and burned, and when I couldn't take the strain anymore, I set my teeth and hauled harder, refused to stop or slow until the sun lowered itself into the sea. I had a family to provide for, and if I caught no fish, they didn't eat. I worked the nets, day in, day out, never considering anything else. What else was there? I had my family, a warm home, a trade I knew.

Then He came.

He strode across the beach, sandals crunching in the sand. The net went slack in my hand, making my brother Andrew grunt in irritation. I didn't care. The man walking towards us on the beach...he was captivating, but I couldn't explain why. I straightened, lifted a hand to shade my eyes from the sun, watched Him approach. Andrew eventually stood up as well and took note of Him. The net dropped to the deck, and the only sound was the wind rippling the sail, fish tails slapping wet wood. He stopped, waves licking at his toes and the hem of his robe. He called out to us, a hand extended in invitation,

"Come, follow me!" His voice was deep and rich, powerful and commanding and gentle. "Follow me and I will make you fishers of men."

The words were strange. We were fishermen, we fished for fish, not people. How could one catch men in a net? I glanced at Andrew, met his gaze for the briefest of moments. Andrew shrugged noncommittally. I looked back to Him, standing at the water's edge, waiting, as if He knew I would go with Him.

The water was cold and jarring in the hot air. I swam until my feet touched lake bottom, waded ashore, donned my robes. He watched me, His eyes a brown that was almost golden, like sunlight through amber; His eyes were the most incredible thing I'd ever seen. His features were the ordinary, rough-hewn planes and angles of a Jew from the backend of nowhere. His hands were calloused like a carpenter's, His hair and beard dark and tangled and thick. His robes were coarse, his sandals old and battered from years of wear. Oh, but His eyes. They were luminous, warm and kind. I stood before Him dripping wet and breathless from my swim, and He stared into my soul, into my heart of hearts, my deepest, secret places, and He knew me intimately. I sensed something emanating from Him, a deep, thrumming, subtle power that seemed woven into His very essence...even now I cannot express in human words what it was like to meet His gaze. It is impossible, I think. Something ineffable stared out from His eyes, something beyond human ken; meeting His gaze is like staring up at the star-washed sky with the infinite millions of stars, like counting the grains of sand, like following the path of a wave across the trackless sea. Staring into His eyes is to stare full into the face of Yahweh. It is terrifying, and yet comforting. He saw the understanding dawning in me, smiled a kind and loving smile which sent a blaze of warmth and joy thrilling through me. He drew me into an embrace. He might have whispered, "*you are mine,*" or I may have heard it in my mind...I cannot say for sure. I stood in awe, rooted to the sand of the beach, Andrew next to me now, equally transfixed.

I knew it, then: this was the Messiah.

That began a three-year odyssey with Him, a lifetime of miracles and joy and pain and wonder packed into three short years. Every day spent with Him was to learn, was to be challenged, every time He looked at you, each slightest glance seared through you, laid bare your every thought and secret and fear and desire and worry; He knew your pride, knew your weakness, knew how to speak to you so gently and softly and powerfully that you would lay at His feet your very soul, could you but grasp it in two calloused hands.

Then, one day, all changed. We were sitting around a table, as we thirteen always did. It was Passover. We broke bread, shared wine, talked and laughed…but we all could feel a tension in the air. It exuded from the Iscariot, Judas. I always had a bad feeling about Judas. He was at the farthest end, near a window, morose and brooding, staring out at the olive trees in the distance, a hot breeze wafting in and fluttering his thick, curling, black hair and trimmed, oiled beard.

Then, words from Him that chilled us all to the bone: "This is my body, which is given for you," holding aloft a loaf of bread, which He broke in two, with solemnity and ceremony. And then, after we had all eaten from the bread, He poured a draught of wine into our cups, and said, "This cup that is poured out for you is the new covenant in my blood."

We drank the wine, stealing glances at each other, asking silently what this all meant. He had spoken before of His death, and we tried to ignore it, tried to pretend that maybe He was wrong, just this once, just about this. Him, die? Please, Yahweh, do not let that day come. He has become a part of us, our Rabbi, our Lord, our friend, our brother, our father...

"But behold," He said slowly, looking into each of our eyes, coming at last to linger upon Judas, "The hand of him who betrays me is with me on the table." We knew, then, that it was real, and that one of us would betray Him to his death.

Later, when the food and wine was all exhausted and we sat on the slopes of the Mount of Olives singing hymns, He turned to me and pierced me with His eyes like luminous pools of shekinah glory and said, "Simon, Simon, behold, Satan has demanded to have you, that he may sift you like wheat, but I have prayed for you that your faith may not fail. And when you have turned again, strengthen your brothers." His words made my hands shake and turned my stomach into a pit of stone.

"Lord!" I protested. "I am ready to go with you both to prison and to death." He had called me, made me anew. I knew then, in that moment, that I would, truly, go anywhere He went, suffer what He suffered. He was the prophesied Messiah...how could I do anything else?

But He looked at me, sadness heavy in His eyes,

and said, "I tell you, Peter, the rooster will not crow this day until you deny three times that you know me." I stared at Him in disbelief, a hollow in my gut, a tremble in my hands. Suddenly, after three years, all was falling apart. I? Deny Him? I vehemently affirmed my willingness to follow Him even unto death, and my words were echoed by the others. But the seed had been planted, and the doubt was there, in the deepest corner of my self. Would I, when the time came, be faithful? Little did I know then how soon would my words be tested.

We went to one of His favorite places to pray, the Garden of Gethsemane. The moon shone high and full, the night air was warm and still. As we walked, I could sense that His spirit was troubled, and I wished I could do something to comfort Him, He who had done so much for so many. He left me with James and John, those wild, thunder-voiced men, left us beneath a spreading tree and went off by Himself to pray as He so often did. We three sat and waited, prayed, conversed…and fell asleep. James, John, and I had sat here waiting for Him a hundred times over the years, all night, sometimes. He could pray for hours without rising from His knees, He could pray from sunset to moonrise through to dawn, without ceasing or tiring. How could we know that this night would be any different?

I awoke to His touch on my shoulder. "Simon? Are you asleep?" He asked, pouring guilt on me. I should have known, should have stayed awake, for Him. "Could you not watch one hour? Watch and pray that you may not enter into temptation. The spirit indeed is willing, but the flesh is weak."

And He went again to pray, leaving us to think on His words. How right He was. We struggled and prayed and fought sleep, but our eyes seemed weighted by anchors, slid inexorably downwards. We nodded off mid-prayer, nudged each other, stood and walked around, slapped our arms, but to no avail. He woke us again, and this time gave us a look which spoke louder than any words. We hung our heads in shame, and He returned to pray, a third time. As He departed, I noticed smears of blood on His brow, as if He had sweat drops of blood rather than salt. This time, we stayed awake mere moments before succumbing to sleep.

"Are you still sleeping and taking your rest?" He asked, anger in his voice this time. He sighed deeply, wiped his brow, turned and gazed into the distance, listening to some voice only He could hear.

"It is enough. The hour has come. The Son of Man is betrayed into the hands of sinners. Rise, let us be going." Even as He spoke the words, Judas crested the hill with a crowd wielding torches and swords and clubs. "See? My betrayer is at hand."

It is a blur, now, a haze of action. The one thing I remember, vividly, is Judas embracing Him, kissing His sweat-sheened cheek. The look He gave Judas was too complex for words, contained too many emotions to be counted or named; foremost, love, and forgiveness mingled in that reproachful, tender, piercing gaze so fraught with the divine glory shining from his eyes, from his very pores.

How dare he? A filthy sicarii, a traitor, a selfish coward, betrays the Messiah, the Promised One, with a kiss? That moment...I see it...Judas at the head of the blood-hungry mob, clean, soft hands gripping His shoulders, lips pale and trembling pressed to His left cheek, then His right, slow and exaggerated...Rabbi, the Messiah, He knew...He clutched Judas's arms for a moment and stared into his eyes, forgiving him, loving him, weeping for him, seeing his death. Judas kissed Him, and the mob went wild.

They seized Him. I saw red, then.

I drew my sword, hacked off the ear of someone in the crowd, sending a spray of blood into the air. Touching the wound with His fingertips, He healed the servant's ear. Words were exchanged, and they led Him away to the high priest. As they departed, I saw one of them toss a small sack to Judas which clinked when he caught it. Judas saw me watching him. He must have seen the hatred in my stare, for the traitor put a hand to his sword, as if to be ready, should I attack him.

I would have, I think, but for the lingering memory of His last words to me: "Put your sword into its sheath; shall I not drink the cup that the Father has given me?"

So Judas turned and slunk away like a frightened dog. I never saw him again, but I heard that they later found him, hung by his own hand from a withered olive tree, his robes soiled, his face tortured and twisted in death and remorse, swinging in the hot winds of Gehenna.

John and I followed them at a distance. With every step I took, I felt my courage, my fierce determination of just a few hours ago draining away. They led Him, hands bound up painfully behind His back, to Annas, and then to Caiaphas, and it was he who questioned Him. John followed further than I dared, being known to the high priest. I might have gone with him, into the interior court where Caiaphas heard trials of the people, but my courage failed me. I stood outside the door, listening to the murmur of voices just beyond the iron-bound wood.

Then it came, that fateful moment. The door squealed open, revealing the pretty face of a servant girl. She motioned for me to enter into the court and led me to a charcoal fire, around which stood a handful of crest-helmeted officers and high-placed servants. The girl glanced over at the dais, where He stood, hands still bound, surrounded by soldiers, then looked quizzically at me.

"You are not one of this man's disciples, are you?" she asked me, gesturing at Him.

Panic swallowed me, overwhelmed me. I was surrounded by the very men seeking to kill Him, the men who had schemed and plotted for His life…how was I to answer? If I said that I am, would they not take me as well? Would they not beat me with their hard fists, kick me with their boots, whip me with their scourges? My flesh crawled, and the truth stuck in my throat.

"I am not." I heard the words drop from my lips like stones.

He turned His head, just then, and looked directly at me. Shame burned in me, but not with more heat than did fear. The crowd around the brazier was examining me now.

"This man is one of them," one said, gesturing at John and at Yeshua.

"No, I am not!" The flickering flames of anger, always so hot, so close within me, grew unbearable.

Could they not just let it go? I was caught up by my denial, now, and I could not go back. Now a third man, an officer who had been with those that arrested Yeshua, looked at me carefully, intently.

"This man was with them, I am certain," he said to his friends gathered around, "for he too is a Galilean."

I cursed, saying, "I do not know what you are talking about!"

At the very moment that the words came from my lips I heard a rooster crow with its loud voice, three times. The blood drained from my face, and my strength fled. I collapsed backwards against a pillar, remembering His words. "…Before the rooster crows three times this day…"

Far across the court Caiaphas' guards were questioning Him, striking Him. When the rooster crowed, He turned His head and met my eyes once more, unblinking through the rivulets of blood that streamed down his face. Images from our years together flashed through me, striking me with lightning force:

Gaiety and joy of a wedding, dancing, laughing, wine by the barrel, tables of food, the radiant bride and glowing groom whirling around each other…a servant whispering in the ear of the father of the bride, gesturing at a wine barrel…Yeshua's mother, sweet young Mary telling Him that they had run out of wine, Yeshua giving gentle instructions… the stunned surprise when the master of the feast tasted the wine…

Baptizing in the Jordan with His wild-eyed cousin John…

Crossing through Samaria, breaking custom and tradition, the woman of ill-repute at the well at midday and the baffling discussion of "living water" and then the crowds of Samaritans milling around Him and seeking the truth with such fervency…

The uncountable thousands of ill and lame that came to Him day in and day out, so trusting, so believing, all healed…men lame since birth standing up and walking away, blind men seeing, dancing and laughing at the beauty of the world around them, lepers casting off their rags and rejoining society…

Crowds of thousands being fed with a few loaves of bread and some fish…

The storm on the Sea of Galilee, rowing furiously with the others, we see a ghostly, radiant figure striding across the waves...our superstitious panic and terror boiling in us until His voice came to us across the water, strong and bold and reassuring...love and trust welling up inside me, stepping out over the side, Thomas clutching at my sleeve in disbelief as I step onto the surface of the water...it felt like the sand on the beach, shifting and slipping under my feet, but ultimately solid as long as my eyes are fixed upon Him, His arms outstretched towards me. A thunderous crash of lightning stole my attention from His luminous face and drew it to the ten foot waves and wind-whipped rain pelting against my face and I began to slip beneath the waves.

"Lord! Help me!" I cried out to Him.

"Oh, you of little faith," He said to me, His voice gentle and reproachful. "Why did you doubt?"

As He speaks, He reaches out a hand—even though mere moments ago He was a dozen feet away across a roiling field of waves—and grasps mine, His grip is firm and strong, He stands legs splayed and back straight, lifting me bodily out of the water with one hand as if I were a child, me, a heavy, thick-muscled fisherman. When He grasps my hand my fear abates instantly and I know I was foolish to doubt Him...He would never abandon me, never allow me to sink beneath the waves.

I slammed back into the present and I saw Him across the courtyard with blood stinging His sinless eyes, loving me silently, perfectly, and I realized that I had failed Him. I stumbled blindly out of the room, heart beating to burst in my chest, crushing guilt in my gut, tears burning my eyes and dripping like liquid shame down my face. I felt gazes on me as I ran sobbing from the court of Caiaphas.

I cannot think on the hours that followed, the scourge ripping His back and sides, the inch-long thorns of the mock-crown digging into His skull, the dull thud of the hammer driving spikes into His wrists...oh my Lord...how can they do this to You? Why do You let this happen? You commanded the very wind and waves to be still, and they subsided, You commanded Lazarus to rise from his days-old grave, and he rose, You can command a host of angels to rescue You, but You remain hung there on the cross, laboring for breath, blood painting You crimson. They mocked You, they jeered at You, those godless, vicious Romans. We disciples sat around your feet, weeping silently. You comforted us with Your eyes even as You died.

The sun stood at its apex, full and burning hot... then shadows crept from beneath the horizon and stole over the land, covered the sun as if to hide the earth and the sun and the moon and the stars from the shame of what mankind was doing to its Savior. The crowds murmured and made signs to ward off evil, knowing in their hearts that something momentous is occurring.

We still did not understand completely why You were doing this. How could we?

You called out in a voice loud enough to reach the farthest of the crowd of thousands who gathered to watch You crucified; You called for Your Father, asked Him why He had forsaken You, and it was then that I begin to glimpse a fragment of what it was You did, there on the cross. I remember the sacrificial lambs on the altar and I saw You there on the cross, and I understood.

It staggered me. I could not completely comprehend it. How could I? Was this for me? Because of my sin? Did I do this to You, Lord? I looked to my left and saw my brother Andrew, and I could tell he as wondering the same thing, and there were James and John and Mary Magdalene, of all us...all thinking—*is this because of me, my Lord?*

The Sea of Tiberias was calm that day, the day He came to us for the last time. We sat on the beach, still full of marvel at His death, and full of wonder at His resurrection. As the day came to an end, however, I simply couldn't sit still anymore.

"I am going fishing," I said.

I didn't know what else to do. I had to do something, anything at all to make sense of the roiling thoughts and emotions that gripped me. I am a simple man, a fisherman: being out on the water has always been a place of solace, a refuge, a place to go and think. The difficult, rhythmic work of casting out the nets and pulling them in has always helped me think. The others all looked at me blankly for a moment. We hadn't fished nearly at all since the day He called us to be "fishers of men," and now, in the midst of events that promised to change the very world, I wanted to go fishing.

"Typical Peter," I heard someone mutter, probably James, son of Zebedee.

But in the end they all put shoulder to hull and shoved off with me. We caught nothing all the night through. I didn't care, I was just glad to be physically exhausted, so tired and sore that I couldn't spend any more energy trying to come to grips with the import of His sacrifice.

Dawn was breaking, our nets were empty, and we about to beach the boats when we heard a voice from shore saying, "Children, do you have any fish?"

"No," we answered.

"Cast the net on the right side of the boat, and you will find some."

We exchanged baffled glances, but did as the figure on the shore had suggested. John and James and I cast the net on the right side and pulled it in, only to find it so heavy with wiggling, flipping, silver-skinned fish that we could not manage it alone. Thomas and Nathanael of Cana lent their strength to the pull. When we had the net in, we slumped to the deck, exhausted. John, however, was peering at the figure intently.

He turned to me, gripping my shoulder, and said, "It is the Lord!"

I turned to look again, and saw that John was right. I jumped in and swam to Him. I do not know how to express with this pen the joy that thrilled through me when I crawled from the water and threw myself into His arms. It really was He! He wrapped his arms around me, and I felt a burst of peace rise up inside me. He held me like a father, and I heard, as I had when first He called me—

"*You are mine.*"

We ate fish and broke bread, and for a little while all was as it had been, before, an early breakfast under the light of dawning day.

Then, He turned to me. "Simon, son of John, do you love me more than these?" He asked, gesturing at the disciples.

How could He ask me that? It broke my heart to hear Him doubt me. I hung my head, knowing I had earned it.

"Yes, Lord; you know that I love you." My voice trembled as I spoke.

"Feed my lambs," He said to me. I opened my mouth to speak a promise, but He spoke over me, gently but firmly. "Simon, son of John, do you love me?"

Now my heart was cracked and falling apart. I loved Him with all that I am. I had failed Him once, but never again. Surely He, the Messiah, could see in me how much I loved Him. Couldn't He?

"Yes Lord; you *know* that I love you." Now my words came thick and slow, heavy and sad.

"Tend my sheep." Once more, I took a breath to speak, but He didn't give me a chance.

"Simon, son of John," He began, a third time, and now tears fell from my eyes, and I struggled to stand from the weight of my grief, could not bear to meet those deep, impossible golden-brown eyes. "Do you love me?"

I couldn't stand any longer; I fell to my knees in the sand, weeping.

I could barely speak, so the words emerged as a broken half-sobbed whisper. "Lord, you know everything, you know that I love you."

Oh, I was broken, then. I struggled to meet His gaze through my tears, and I saw…I saw so much there, in His eyes, such infinite love, such forgiveness, and I understood with lightning-swift clarity why He had asked me, three times, if I loved Him. Each time, He was forgiving me for each denial. Each time He asked me, "Do you love me?" He was wrapping His arms around me and whispering in my ear, "*You are mine*," and making me eternally His.

"Feed my sheep," He said, once more. His next words reverberated in my soul, echoed deeply. "Truly, truly I say to you, when you were young, you used to dress yourself and walk wherever you wanted, but when you are old, you will stretch out your hands, and another will dress you and carry you where you do not want to go."

To the last, speaking in riddles. The parables, the

stories, the lessons, they seemed so clear, but always there was an element that we knew we were missing. What did this mean? It seemed frighteningly like a prophesy of my death. At last, He turned to me and told me to follow Him...

And I followed Him across the whole earth, speaking of Him, preaching His message with words given to me as I needed them. I followed. I kept the faith in all circumstances. I vowed that I would never again fail or deny Him, no matter the cost.

So now, here I sit in a jail cell beneath the Holy City of Jerusalem, waiting for the guards to take me up and take from me the ultimate cost. I am old now, and tired. I do not go willingly, for I would spend my last breath, my last shred of strength bringing the good news of His life, death, and resurrection to all people. I was never so at home as when aboard a ship plying the seas, rolling with the swells, climbing up and crashing down, sail bellied out with a strong wind, a new place drawing near, new people in need of His joy. He has been beside me all the while, down every road, across every sea, whispering to me, "*you are mine*," and "*follow me*."

I am His, so I followed Him.

I realize now what His very first words to me meant. I never understood it until this moment, as the guard's key turns in the lock.

"Come," He commanded, "and I will make you fishers of men."

I put aside, then, the nets and ceased casting for fish. I took up a net of His message and cast it for men. He truly made of me a fisher of men.

They will stretch out my hands, and dress me, and carry me where I do not wish to go...I know this. I am afraid. This will be my last test, my last sermon.
Lord, you know I love you.

They took him, one at each arm, half dragged him up the mossy stone steps into daylight, dressed him, brought him before a tribunal.

"Deny this madness," they commanded him. "Deny this false prophet, this Yeshua of Nazareth. Deny Him, and we will set you free."

They stood before him, resplendent in polished silver mail, bright crimson cloaks and crested helmets held smartly beneath arms, pila gripped in gloved hands. He was old, bent, gray, wrinkled, but he bore the marks of a man once mighty. He pulled himself erect, grimacing with the effort, spread his feet apart as he had for a lifetime to balance against the rolling deck of a fishing boat. He closed his eyes, briefly, lips forming a silent prayer. He opened his mouth to speak, and when he did so, he gained new life, imbued with a spirit of vitality and eloquence. He spoke one last message to a crowd gathered to watch the execution of this man, Peter, who had walked with the Christ.

"Yeshua of Nazareth," Peter said in a voice preternaturally powerful, carrying to the farthest spectator, "was the Messiah. I walked with Him, I loved Him, and I served Him all my life. I will not deny Him."

Peter then spoke the Good News, and not one of the Romans interrupted him. They all stood spellbound as he spoke, and there was more than one stone heart softened and stirred in that place.

The centurion gave a curt command, and the legionnaires stretched him upon the cross, stripped him, hammered the spikes through parchment-thin skin and purple-veined wrists, lifted him—hanging him, upon his own request, upside down—and watched him die.

At the last he looked to Heaven as if seeing a dear friend once more. "Lord, you know everything," he said, "you know that I love you."

And he gave up his spirit.

FROM THE FICTION:
Poetry & Lyrics

Falling Into You: Cotton's Lullaby

Quiet your crying voice, lost child.
Let no plea for comfort pass your lips.
You're okay, now.
You're okay, now.
Don't cry anymore, dry your eyes.
Roll the pain away,
put it down on the ground
and leave it for the birds.
Suffer no more, lost child.
Stand and take the road,
move on and seal the hurt behind the miles.
It's not all right, it's not okay.
I know, I know.
The night is long, it's dark and cruel.
I know, I know.
You're not alone. You're not alone.
You are loved. You are held.
Quiet your crying voice, lost child.
You're okay, now.
You're okay, now.
Just hold on, one more day.
Just hold on, one more hour.
Someone will come for you.
Someone will hold you close.
I know, I know.

It's not okay, it's not all right.
But if you just hold on,
One more day, one more hour.
It will be.
It will be.

Falling Into You

All my life it seems
I've been falling,
Failing,
Flailing,
Barely keeping my head above water.
And then one day
I saw you
Standing beneath a spreading tree,
Refusing to weep.
But even then I saw
The weight of pain hiding in your eyes,
And I wished then,
There beneath that tree,
To take it all away.
But I had no words to heal you.
I had no words to heal myself.
And now that Fate has intervened,
Conspired to draw us together,
Despite the years between us,
Despite the weight of pain
Behind both our eyes,
Despite the ghosts trailing all around us
Like a fog of haunting souls,
I'm still trying to find the words to heal you,
To take your pain and make it all my own

So your beautiful eyes can smile,
So you can be at peace.
And now that Fate has intervened,
Conspired to draw us together,
I can't resist the lure of your eyes,
The temptation of your beauty,
The siren song of your voice
Whispering my name
In the dark comfort between my sheets.
I can't resist you, baby,
Because I'm falling still,
I'm falling into you

Falling Into You: Colton's Farewell

You've never had a name.
You've never had a face.
A thousand breaths you'll never take
Echo in my mind,
My child, child, child.
The questions blink like stars,
Numberless in the night sky.
Did you dream?
Did you have a soul?
Who could you have been?
You've never known my arms,
You've never known your mother's arms,
My child, child, child.
I'll dream for you,
I'll breathe for you,
I'll question God for you,
I'll shake my fists and scream and cry for you.
This song is for you,
It's all I've got.
It doesn't give you a name.
It doesn't give you a face.
But it's all I've got to give.
All my love is in these words I sing,
In each haunted note from my guitar,
My child, child, child.

You're not gone,
Because you never were.
But that doesn't mean
You passed unloved.
It doesn't mean you're forgotten,
Unborn child, child, child.
I bury you
With this song.
I mourn you
With this song.

Falling Into Us: The Calculus of Boredom

The average rate of change
Seems to define my axis of rotation.
The area of an ellipse
Definitely defines the constant term
Of my life.
My daily pattern of being
Is the end behavior of my
Bounded function.
Degenerate, derivative, differential,
Essential discontinuity,
Explicit differentiation,
Explicit function:
Exponential Decay.
I have no me,
I have only
The conditional convergence
Of their constant term
Of continuous function
Of disapproval.
Each decision seems to be
Part of a chain rule,
An annulus,
Or,
The region between two concentric circles which have different radii; or,

In other words…
My
Fucking
Parents.

Falling Into Us: Anywhere But Here

Trees wave and tease
Blown in the long free breeze
Urging me out and into the blue
Into the sunlit green spaces
Where no words trip over clumsy tongues
Where no tensions drip like rain from eaves
I don't even wish I was a bird
I only wish I was out there
Walking in the grass or climbing in the trees
Heated by the sun or chilled by the wind
or wet in the rain
Anywhere but here
Chained to this stagnant shore
A prisoner of perfection
An enemy of state
For no more crime than being
A teenaged girl
In like with a teenaged boy
For no more crime than driving
In lazy dusty endless circles
Listening to country songs
And my own nervous heartbeat
My pulse pounding and my nerves twanging
Like the banjos on the radio
I can't even shout my anger

Can't even scream my frustration
Can't even curse
It would only come out a jumble
"Fu—fu-fu-fuck you!"
Fu fu fu fu
Bu bu bu bu
Duh duh duh
Childish stumbling words
Tripping syllables and slippery syntactic screwups
That's me
The silent girl
The stutterer
The prisoner
The smart girl
The valedictorian scribbling maledictions to no one

Falling into us: Ghostkiss

You're not here, and I'm not there
I'm a girl, alone in her room
And you're a myth
A possible future
A ghost of my desires to come
I breathe slowly and close my eyes
Tilt my face to the ceiling
And wait for the kiss
Of ghostly lips on flesh
Dream mouth on real
Fantasy tongue tasting mine
Tantalizing and imagined
Because I wonder
What a kiss is
How lips taste
How a tongue feels
Will I know what to do
Without being shown?
A more worrisome question arises
One unique to me:
Can you stutter, in a kiss?
Can you fumble
In the throes of desire?
You're just a ghost
A neverknown fraction of what-if

And you cannot teach me what I wish to know
Until you become real
And kiss me and kiss me and kiss me

Falling Into Us

How do I resist the gentle need in your eyes?
I don't
I can't
Not when that same heartdeep,
soulspearing desperation is rooted within me
Tendrils of sunhot want
wrapping around my soul
Like ivy up a brick wall
God, your eyes
Greener than summer grass
Greener than moss and sunlit jade
Sharper than obsidian
Gentler than clouds and feathertouch
They burn into me when we kiss
They scorch me when I score your skin
with trembling fingernails
And I know, I know, I know
All too well
Where all this is going
I've seen it happen in my dreams
I've seen it play out
in the steam-wreathed privacy of my shower
Where I touch my hot, shivering flesh
And imagine it's you
Wish it was you

It's been you
But not like we both want
And that's where it's going
We're dancing on the edge of a knife
And I want to fall over
With you
But I can't help being a little afraid
Of the adulthood lying on the other side
I'm afraid of what we can't take back
Of giving away that last piece of my girlhood
Even to you
And yeah, I know, I love you
And yeah, I know, you love me
But yeah, I know, we're still just kids
We're as close to junior high as we are college
As close to twelve as we are twenty
And I don't want to regret a thing
God, I'm so confused
And the only time I'm sure of anything
Is when you're kissing me
And then it's all too easy to forget
Everything but the way I feel
The way you feel so close to me
And I can't help wondering
If that's the smartest time to make such decisions
Exactly because I get so lost
Because it feels so much like falling
Into love
Into you and me

Being in love is scary
So much like falling
A frightening descent into
Beautiful madness
Yes, you and me
We're
Falling into Us
And I don't dare stop the fall
Because I need it far too much

Falling Into Us: A Thin Red line

You looked so guilty
When I walked in
Your eyes were haunted
Your hands trembling
And I watched a thin red line
blossom on your wrist
An evil scarlet flower
Trailing skeins of leaked pain down your arm
So easily wiped away
Covered over
Hidden
By bandages and lies and shirtsleeves
Glossed over by blasé reassurances
That it helped
Somehow
As if gashes gouged in your skin
Could take away the grief
You looked so guilty
When I walked in
Jumping up from giving yourself scars
And I wonder
If my bought silence
Will be your death
And I wonder
If the vault of my soul

Can hold any more secrets
Any more hidden sins
All this wells up on your skin
Bleeds out from
A thin red line
Cut into your wrist

Falling Into Us: For Ben

I don't mourn you,
Brother.
I don't grieve for you.
If there is thought
Or grief
Or love
After this life,
Then you're watching,
And you're mad at us.
You're angry,
But you're at peace.
I don't mourn you,
Brother.
But I miss you.
I wish you hadn't left,
Hadn't removed yourself
So violently
From us all.
From me.
I miss you.
I love you,
Brother.
And I'm sorry.
I'm sorry I didn't love you
More.

I can't say if you're in a better place.
Maybe that's a myth we tell
To comfort ourselves.
There's too much to say,
And not enough words
For me to say it all.
If you're here,
If you're listening,
Then I hope you find,
In whatever place you're in,
What you were looking for.

Falling Into Us: For Kylie

You've got your momma's eyes, you know,
My little baby girl.
You take a breath and you capture my heart.
You've got your momma's nose, you know,
My little baby girl.
You clutch my fingers with all your strength,
And you hold my soul in your tiny hands.
I dreamed of you,
My little baby girl.
I dreamed of you,
Every single night for nine long months.
But I never dreamed
You'd steal me with your eyes
So much like your momma's.
Every father has a ghost, you know,
My little baby girl,
He's haunted by all the things he could do wrong.
So I can only hold you close
And hope I do it right,
Hope I love you enough
Hope I give you everything you deserve.
I dreamed of you, you know,
My little baby girl
With your momma's eyes.
I dream of you still,

I dream of what you'll be
And what you'll do.
I dream of seeing your first steps and
Hearing your first word.
I have another ghost,
Every father's subtle fear,
The day we blink you're behind the wheel,
Blink again and you're on a date
With a boy we can't stand,
Blink again and you're graduating,
Blink again I'm walking you down the aisle.
So don't grow up,
My little baby girl.
Stay small and warm and soft,
And fitting in my arms
Falling asleep to my singing voice.
Don't grow up
My little baby girl.
At least not too fast.

Falling Under:
Kylie's Song – Only the Everything

Flaws are the fabric of a soul,
And yours are deep,
Twisted thick into the damask of who you are
But I see past the flaws.
I'm not blind, I'm not blind, I'm not blind.
It may not be love,
It may be love,
It may be something else,
Maybe something in between love and not
I don't know, and I wouldn't be
writing these words if I did,
I wouldn't be lost and drifting and scribbling
at three in the morning,
If I did.
So your flaws, the tangled web
of secrets and sins and scars,
They're you, you, you,
And I see you,
I see you
I see you.
You hide behind the hard and impenetrable flesh
of your scars,
You hide behind the things that make you human,

And that's all I want,
The human, the inside and the outside
the good and the bad,
It's all I want,
The everything,
The ugly and beautiful and the gray in between
All mixed up like a slush and a slurry of pieces.
I don't miss the way you look at me,
The disbelief that I could see through the mask you wear,
The truth you wield like a disguise,
The weapons of your fists
and the ink of your tattoos,
They're you, you, you
But not the whole, not the entirety
not the everything,
And don't you know,
Don't you see,
Can't you understand
that all I want
Is only the everything,
Only the everything,
Only the everything
That is you.

Falling Under: Kylie & Oz's Duet - Kylie

Watching this unfold,
watching hours become moments
Become weeks become days,
It's all a game, all a trick,
hopeless despite my intents.
I'm watching you close
and I'm lost in your maze
I can't find my way,
don't have a map of your terrain.
I'm trying and I'm diving in,
but I'm caught up in your pain,
I'm lost and I'm looking for you,
but your secrets are a stain,
They leave a shadow
on the clarity of what I feel.
Your secrets and the hidden scars
Are holes in your skin,
but light shines through,
bright as stars

Falling Under: Kylie & Oz's Duet – Oz

You wish you knew me,
You wish you could see me,
Maybe you think a few kind words will free me.
But darling, they won't.
Darling, they won't.
Your eyes betray your fear,
You come close to me, draw near,
Afraid, maybe curious,
maybe thinking you can save me.
But darling, you can't.
Darling, you can't.
Your world and mine,
They're a million miles apart,
And baby, maybe you think
you can bridge the gap,
But darling, you can't.
Darling, you can't.

Falling Under: Not Your Me

A lifetime of you and me
A lifetime of here we are
Day in day out of just be
Of talking free
Of easy and slow
But there have always been
Moments of what if
Moments of does he doesn't he
Can we, could we, should we
Dismiss it, ignore it, pretend
I never had those thoughts
Put the wishes to an end
Live and breathe and move
Find a brand-new groove
Keep going and just be
You and me
Day in day out
You and me
Day in day out
And then like a flash flood
Like a sudden slide of mud
I'm in love with someone else
And you and me aren't you and me
You're you
And I'm someone else

You're not you
And I'm still me
And who are we
Who are we
Where's the we
We used to be
Discover does he doesn't he
Has always been does he
Only I never knew
And the moments are too few
Too late
The time is gone
Long ago and long
And my heart is full of someone else
But you're still you
I'm still me
There's just no longer any we
Because your heart is full of me
But I'm not that me
Your me
I'm his me
And you want what can't ever be
But you still look at me
As if all the we
and all the what if
and all the as if
and all the used to be
Could ever add up to
A new you and me

And I don't want this guilt
I don't want this guilt
I don't want you to wish
Don't want you to keep hoping
Keep holding on and holding out
I want you to find your own someone else
Your own brand-new you and me
Your own fresh lifetime of here we are now
Day in day out
Of talking free
Easy and slow
I wish you could know
How much I miss you
How much I miss
The way we used to be
But god can't you see
I'm no longer that girl
I'm not your me
I'm not your me.

Falling Under

All my life it seems
I've been barely keeping
My head above the water
And then I saw you
You saw all the pain
Hiding in my eyes
And you wanted
To take it away

But I had no words for you
'Cause I was falling under

And I am falling, falling under with you
I can't resist you, baby
I'm falling, falling under with you
Your love healed me

Fate has intervened
Conspiring to draw us close together
And tangle our lives
The siren of your song
And the music of your heart is calling
Whispering my name

And now I have the words for you
'Cause I'm falling under with you

Now I'm falling, falling under with you
I can't resist you, baby
I am falling, falling under with you
And I'm falling still
I'm falling still

Now that fate has intervened
And drawn us close together
Past our fears and all the pain
Behind our eyes
Despite the ghosts trailing around us
Like a fog of haunting souls
You're still trying hard to heal me
To take my pain and make it yours
Your beautiful eyes are smiling
Into mine

Now I'm falling, falling under with you
I can't resist you, baby
I am falling, falling under with you
And I'm falling still
I'm falling still
I'm falling still
Falling under with you.

Falling Away: Only The Moon

It's a long, long road to walk alone,
A dark and winding path that I must roam,
And I've only the moon to keep me company,
Only the moon to watch me on my way.
A broken heart chose this path,
A heart cracked by grief sent me this way.
And I've only the moon to sing me
down the road,
Only the moon to warm me in this cold.
My feet falter, my tears drip,
Fall like rain, so much salt on my lip.
And I've only the moon to watch me weep,
Only the moon my secrets to keep.
I left you there,
I knew your heart,
And I left you there,
With only the moon to light your way,
With only the moon to hear you say,
Come back, come back, come back.
Oh, oh, oh, oh,
I've only the moon to sing me down the road,
Only the moon to warm me in the cold,
Only the moon to watch me weep,
Only the moon my secrets to keep,
Only the moon to hear me say,
Come back, come back, come back…

Falling Away: Don't Need Love

I don't need to love, you know,
Don't need the heartache,
Don't need the high or the low,
Don't need anyone but me,
I don't need to cling to you
Late at night, through the stars as they sing,
Don't need love, old or new.
I just need me.
Because I'm all there is,
I'm all right,
I'm all right,
And I don't need love.
I've ached and I've hurt and I've cried,
I've loved and lost and love has died,
I've learned the lessons, and now I know,
I don't need to love,
Don't need the high or the low,
Don't need anyone but me
Because I'm all there is,
And I'm all right,
I'm all right.

Falling Away: Perfect Pain

Oh god, it's like a hole,
Ripped into my chest,
And I can see my bones,
Each and every one.
My bones, they prick and stab,
Poke and slash,
And I wish sometimes
That I was dead,
Lying on a slab.
If I was dead, I wouldn't have to feel this,
I wouldn't have to know this pain,
Wouldn't have to bear it,
Because this kind of pain,
You can't help but wear it,
When it cuts you deep,
Slashes at your heart, and tears it.
Oh god, it's like a hole,
Tearing me in two,
And from that wound
Bleeds my life,
Bleeds my heart,
Bleeds the last of my innocence.
From that hole bleeds my soul,
Bleeds my soul,
Thus bleeds my soul.

You see it, all this blood?
Of course you don't,
Because it only bleeds within,
It's not the blood that's red,
The blood that's hot and wet.
It's the blood of will,
Blood of peace,
Blood of innocence.
You can't see this blood,
Can you?
Because it's only on my soul.
I wish, I wish, I wish,
Oh god I wish I could show it to you,
So you could see the hole you left,
When you forced me to the floor.
So you could see
what perfect pain you wrought,
Such perfect pain,
Created by your drunken hands,
By your brutal breath,
Hot on me in that dark,
You caused such agony,
Such perfect pain,
That perfect pain,
That awful, perfect pain.

Falling Away: Only For Tonight

I don't know you,
But that's okay.
I don't know you,
But I will, soon enough.
There's just the beat of the music,
And the beat of my heart,
And the touch of your hands,
And the spark on our tongues.
That's all we need,
If only for tonight,
If only till the hot sun rises,
If only till you see my flaws,
And you see my makeup
Streaked and smeared,
Only till you see me fix my skirt
And forget to write your number down.
It's enough for tonight,
If only till the buzz wears off,
Till the whiskey all runs out.
I don't need tomorrow,
I don't need to know you,
I don't need your name,
Or even one of your secrets,
I only need you for tonight.
I only need the beat of my heart,

And the touch of your hands,
I only need the spark on our tongues.
I only need the whiskey of your kiss
And the silence as we fumble our way
to sunrise.
It's enough, it's enough,
It's got to be enough,
Because honey, it's all we'll ever get,
It's all I have to give,
If only for tonight.
You get me till the hot sun rises,
Till the whiskey runs dry,
Till I fix my skirt,
And forget to write your number down,
Till I wash the makeup off,
Till I change my skirt,
If only until I go out tomorrow night,
And sing this song again.
Because honey, I only need tonight,
And I don't need your name,
I just need the spark on our tongues
And the beat of the music,
And the whiskey of your kiss,
Only for tonight.

Falling Away: Forgive Me

Forgive me, forgive me…forgive me,
But I just can't get those words out,
Those two little words, can't set 'em free,
Forgive me, forgive me, forgive me,
I should be able to say it, should be easy,
But those words, they get stuck
And anyway it's not like you give a fuck
If I say I'm sorry, they're just words,
two little words,
That mean so little,
Too little, too late,
And they just can't erase the hate
I pile on myself,
Can't bury the guilt I keep on my shelf,
Can't bring down these walls,
Can't tear down these halls,
Even if I beg you on bended knee,
Forgive me, forgive me,
Forgive me,
I should be able to say it,
But those words just get stuck,
And anyway it's not like you give a fuck,
And it's just my luck,
You'd forgive me, you'd forgive me
Like it's just that easy,

Because we all know the truth,
We all know the hardest part,
The thing that's really an art,
Is when I say forgive me, forgive me,
Forgive me,
Is to say it to myself,
To take the guilt off the shelf,
To bring down my walls,
To tear down the halls,
To beg myself, to plead with my own soul,
Forgive me, forgive me, forgive me.

Falling Away

An instant, oh just a single fragment
Is all it takes to turn my long lament
Into a song of dizzy joy,
To shake the sorrow from my bones
And know that I am not alone.
An instant, oh just a single glance
Just a single touch, by chance,
And I know I'm not alone.

All the sorrow, love of mine,
Oh, you take it all away,
You send it with the wind,
All the sorrow, love of mine,
All the sadness, oh, all the guilt,
The tower of my solitude,
It's falling, falling, falling away.

An instant, oh, just a single fragment
Is all it takes to turn my long lament
Into a song of love,
To shake the sorrow from my bones,
And know that I am not alone.
An instant, oh, just a single kiss
And I'm raptured, oh, oh,
I'm drowning in your bliss,

My senses drown in the brown of your eyes
And oh, all the history is buried by our sighs,
All the sorrow and oh, all the guilt,
It's all pulled down, down
with all the walls I built,

It's falling, falling, falling away,
Love of mine, oh
Love of mine, oh,
I'm falling, falling away, away,
I'm sinking into you, oh, and forever I'll stay,
So take me now and lay me down,
Fall with me, oh,
Sing with me, sigh with me, lie with me,

Because it's you and only you,
Whose kiss, whose touch, whose love,
Who with a single word, oh, a single glance,
Can change the vagaries of chance,
Can sweep me up and make me dance,
Can shake the sorrow from my bones,
Show me that I'm not alone,

With just an instant, oh,
With just a kiss and I know,
It's going to be okay, oh, going to be okay,
Because
We're falling, falling, falling away.

The Long Way Home:

THE SELKIE AND THE SEA

A short story by
Christian St. Pierre

Brighid considered herself a widow. There was no news for certain, but then, there probably never would be. That was just the way of things. Her husband Calum had taken a berth aboard a whaler two years ago, and hadn't returned. Nor had he sent any letters—which wasn't all that surprising given that Calum could barely write his own name—but on the voyages before this one he'd at least sent money, and sometimes a note in the hand of someone to whom he'd dictated his thoughts. Perhaps even a parcel containing a bolt of calico or lace as a token of his regards.

Two years, now, and not a word. Ships came and went month by month, some with news from other men in the village: Michael O'Halloran had taken ill with malaria, and was stranded in Barbados until he'd healed; Sean Moran had lost his leg and was bound for home on a company ship; Tommy Dooley had been lost at sea and was thought dead. No news of Calum, however.

So Brighid carried on as best she could, alone.

Herded the sheep and goats from pasture to pasture, fed the chickens and collected and sold the eggs at market, sheared wool at the appropriate season, milked the goats and made cheese, mended fences.

And watched the sea.

She had a ritual, performed daily. Once the day's work was done, she would follow the narrow path from the field behind her little home and over the dunes and through the tall dune grass waving in the ever-blowing wind and down to the sea. She would kick off her shoes when the trail ended at the sand, and she'd pause there, digging her bare toes into the cool sand, wiggle her heels, fill her lungs, and let her hair down. The wind would play with her hair, blowing the long red locks this way and that, draping a strand across her eye. The wind would play with her skirt, too, flirty and presumptuous, tugging at it, pressing the linen against her thighs. It would pry at the edges of her sweater and mould the sweat-damp cotton against the mounds of her breasts. Then Brighid would gather the hem of her skirt up to her knees and knot it there to leave her legs bare; there was no one to see, after all, since Calum had built their home miles from the village, right up against the sea on the west, in a green sward boxed in by hills to the east and south, accessible only by a narrow, rocky path to the north. It was a place of solitude and solace, their little farm. Far from any prying eyes. And so Brighid would tie her skirt up indecently high, because only the gulls were there to see the white flash of her thighs and calves.

She would traipse down to the water's edge, and let it tickle her toes. Her eyes would scan the horizon, east to west, watching for sails, praying that the next she saw would have word of Calum, but knowing in her breast that no ship would come, not with word of Calum. But still she spent her evenings at the sea's edge, hoping. Letting the sea foam drag at her ankles, biting achingly cold on her bones. If she went too deep, calf-deep, as she sometimes did, on warm days, her ankle would throb, a reminder of the time she broke it as a girl, chasing a sheep away from a cliff's edge.

She liked the ache, secretly. The cold was bracing. Sometimes, in the depths of her heart, she wished she had the courage to strip all of her clothes off and delve beneath the waves and let that delicious icy ache spread through her whole body. She never did, though. She'd gone thigh-deep, once. She'd had to hike her skirts up to her waist, and had stopped when the water began to lap and lick in an indecently intimate way. She'd splashed ashore trembling, and had made her cook fire in the hearth that evening especially hot.

Day after day, Brighid went down to the sea, waded in the cold brine, and watched the horizon.

And then, one evening, after a day of particularly brutal rain, Brighid as usual followed her path down to the sea, kicked off her shoes, and waded ankle-deep in the icy water. She followed the shoreline a ways, kicking at the waves, her hair let down to flutter behind her like a copper banner. The wind was sharp and strong, pressing her clothes hard against her body, tossing her hair this way and that, more aggressive than flirtatious. And the sea was full of ire, still, sending an occasional wave crashing against the shore in a spray of cold white foam to surge calf-deep. So Brighid tied her skirt up around her thighs to keep the hem dry, and followed the shoreline. She whispered a prayer to Brendan moccu Altae, saint of the seas and mariners, more as an idle pastime and a vaguely remembered habit than real faith in the saint to bring her husband back.

Hear my prayer, Saint Brendan, she prayed. *Assuage my loneliness. Return him to me. Show mercy to me.*

The whispered words upon her lips, she felt the wind scraping in from the sea, harsh and cold, sending shivers down her spine, and the sea roared and crashed, and waves licked at her calves like a cold tongue. She continued along the shore, mindless of distance, heedless of time.

Her eyes cast down, following only the restless advance and retreat of the surf, she was thus startled when she heard a footstep in the wet sand. She looked up just in time to see the nude form of a man, turning from her and leaping into the sea, a bounding splashing step, a second, a third, knees driving high, taut dark buttocks driving him powerfully into the surf, and then he dove, a graceful shallow plunge headfirst into the waves. Her vision of him was brief, but his form was immediately imprinted upon her mind. He was tall, taller than Calum even, who stood head and shoulders taller than most men in the village. His back had been muscled and firm, his shoulders broad and his waist narrow, with the powerful legs and buttocks of an athlete or warrior. His hair had been long, unkempt, wild, wet and dark black and pasted to his spine and shoulder blades.

Brighid stared after him, waiting for him to surface, to rise up and gasp and splutter at the cold, to poke his head up over the waves and glance back at her. For long, long minutes Brighid stood and stared, with the cold brine pooling around her ankles with the inrush of the evening tide. Longer than anyone could hold a single breath. Had he drowned? Brighid moved deeper into the water, sucking in a deep breath at the icy ache at her knees.

And then, far, far in the distance, she saw a shape breasting the water, leaving a V-shaped wake in the white-capped waves; a head, perhaps, ducking and rising back above the surface. Too far to tell for sure, but it could have been him. Or perhaps it was just a seal, startled away by his presence—they liked this stretch of beach, Brighid knew, because it was remote and rocky and contained tide pools where fish became trapped, and fishermen rarely ventured here, preferring other easier places to ply their trade. It suited Brighid, and it suited the seals as well, and she often saw them sunning their bellies in the distance, and as she approached they would bark and splash into the waves and surface only when they'd put a healthy distance behind them.

A seal, or a man? From this distance, there was no way to know.

Brighid was cold, now. The wind still blew damp with the day's rain, and the surf was rough and angry, dampening her skirts even bound up as they were, and now her legs ached with the dull insistent throb of the sea's icy teeth. She trudged through the encroaching tide into the damp hard-packed dark brown sand and then up to the dry tan sand, where her feet sank in and were engulfed by the relatively warm grit. She looked back, but the sea was empty again, except for the omnipresent gulls, hawing and wheeling, skreeing and floating head-on in the wind, riding the currents and crying their discordant discourse.

She went home and stirred the fire into blazing heat to warm the ache from her bones, and ate the last of the mutton stew; she'd have to make more for dinner the next few days, which meant slaughtering another sheep, a chore she loathed. Her mind wandered, that night, as she drifted off to sleep.

Calum was floating beside her. She was lost in the waves, drowning. She could feel her hair billowing in the sea currents, but she could breathe and he couldn't. He was sinking out of reach, and she was weeping, soundless under the surface of the waves. Above, a storm raged; she saw the lightning flash, saw the vengeful churn of the sea. Calum reached for her, his fine blond hair a yellow cloud, his eyes all black, no white, no pupil, no life, and his mouth worked, closed and opened, speaking, pleading, and his hand reached, reached, reached for her but never could she grasp his hand and pull him to safety.

Brighid woke as Calum drifted down into the inky depths, woke screaming his name, gasping in the dark silence of predawn.

There would be no more sleep, she knew; she would meet him in the waves again if she tried to sleep. Instead, she lit her lamp and mended rends in dresses and darned the holes in her stockings and bided her time until it was light enough to milk the goats and put them and the sheep out to pasture. All the while, her mind was on the dream she'd had. Calum, reaching for her, sinking into the depths. As much a confirmation of his demise as she was likely to get, although she would never have admitted to such superstition out loud.

Her nearest neighbor, taciturn old Mr. Malloy, had traded her some lobster traps for a few pails of milk, and had shown her where and how to place them, so she brought a large pail down to the shoals with her skirts tied high and her hair braided tightly to prevent tangles in the mischievous wind of the morning. Scrambling across the rocks and down into the thigh-deep pools, she hauled up the first trap, and found a trio of angry, tentacle-waving crustaceans therein; the next few traps were empty, and the last pair held four more each, which made for a tidy enough haul that Brighid made a mental note to bring Mr. Malloy some of her goat cheese, which was nearly done aging.

With her lobsters ticking and clacking and

climbing claw-upon-eyestalk in the bucket, Brighid picked her way carefully back across the spit of surf-slick rocks and then slid down a sandy embankment to the beach proper, and there pulled up short, breathless in fright and shock.

A monstrous harbour seal was beached not half a dozen paces away, dark eyes wet and fixed on her, whiskers twitching. It was on its side, its tail in the surf, a flipper in the air waving listlessly. She set down her pail of lobsters and inched toward the seal; he—the mighty beast was a he, she was somehow certain—was staring at her. She could feel his gaze.

Urrrr—Ur-ur-ur-urrrrrr. He sounded...weak. Troubled. In pain.

Brighid—fearful of the size of the beast, which was well over six feet in length and weighed several hundred pounds, easily—inched incrementally closer, keeping her eyes on his. His wet skin was mottled dark gray, speckled with a spray of white spots around the base of his tail.

A few inches closer, and Brighid was nearly close enough to touch him, should she reach out her hand. He growled again, a throaty rumbling that was somehow non-threatening. His eyes were round limpid pools of ink, shining and glimmering with emotion and intelligence. Closer and closer yet, and the seal did not move. Brighid knew she was being foolish. Seals were ungentle creatures, despite their playful reputation. Males could be territorial, and downright dangerous if threatened, and this close, Brighid was at his mercy. But his bark as she laid a trembling palm on the top of his neck was pained, a beseeching murmur. His flipper waved again, flopping listlessly back and forth.

Brighid, shaking all over, moving slowly and keeping a wary, cautious eye on the beast, shuffled toward the wavering flipper. The seal shifted abruptly, rolling away from her, causing Brighid to yelp in fright and stumble away. But he made no other move so she crouched beside him, one hand on his slick, soft wet skin, trailing across his body as she examined him. There, underneath his flipper, was a huge, wicked, curved fishhook, all of a foot long, speared directly through his flipper and skin near his body. A nasty barb at the tip prevented the horrible hook from sliding out.

"Oh my, you poor creature," Brighid crooned. "You've been hooked, haven't you?"

Urrrrr...urr-ur-urk.

"You just wait here, won't you? I have just the thing." She patted his thick neck. "I swear you can understand me, can't you? I'll be right back. Don't you move, all right? I'll help you."

Urrrrrrk-ur-ur-ur.

Once again, his bark felt eerily and even preternaturally like an intentional response. Brighid shrugged off the shiver that shuddered down her spine. She snatched a lobster from the pail and tossed it toward the seal, who barked again, excitedly, and flopped toward the snapping, clicking crustacean, and then fierce canine teeth crunched and the lobster became a meal for the seal.

Brighid shuddered at the sudden violence, but then turned away and ran as fast as she could up the shore toward her home. Up the dunes she scrambled, dune grass slicing and prickling and stabbing at her calves. At the back of her little house—a small, snug, squat structure of piled stones and hand-hewn timbers and jagged, overlapping, mortared hunks of slate for the roof, built with love and skill by Calum and his eight brothers, most of whom lived several counties over, now, and couldn't spare a month's journey to help her—sat a huge old wooden chest, the wood rotting and the metal straps rusting. Within were Calum's old tools: a hammer, an adze, a saw, a handful of nails... and a pair of thick-handled, blunt-jawed pliers, with enough of a blade to the jaw that it should probably snip through the barbed tip of the hook, if she could summon the strength.

Along with the pliers, she fetched a strip of cloth and a jar of salve, and then jogged back down to the beach where the seal had been. Upon her return, she discovered that the seal had, in her absence, knocked over her pail of lobsters and devoured them all.

"Oh, you naughty beast!" She scolded, with an amused huff. "You've eaten all my lobsters! That was meant to be my dinner, you know. Not very nice of you, was it?"

Ur-ur-ur-ur. If a seal's bark could be said to be almost apologetic, that one was.

"Well, no matter. I'll rebait them later, and catch more. I suppose you need them more than me, anyway." She knelt beside him once more, set the cloth and salve to one side, and grasped the pliers in both hands, pinching the tip of the hook just beneath the barb in the heavy, bladed jaws. "Now, hold still, yeah? I don't want to hurt you further. I may not be strong enough to cut through this."

She applied all the pressure she was capable of, but the pliers only bit in the slightest amount. Letting go, Brighid sank back into the sand with a huff. A moment's rest, and then she bore down once more, grunting with exertion, feeling the hook give just a touch, this time. Unclenching the pliers, she examined her progress: she'd managed a pair of fairly deep divots on either side, but wasn't even halfway through, yet. She rotated the pliers so the blades would sink into new spots, and bore down again. And again. Rotate back to the original location, and she squeezed the handle with all her might, sweat dripping from her nose, hands aching, the seal watching, breathing, not making a sound or moving a muscle.

"Good boy," Brighid murmured to him. "Nearly there, now. A bit more and we'll have it, won't we? Keep still a moment more, and I'll have you patched up good as new."

It was more than a moment or two, but eventually and with much groaning exertion, Brighid managed to snap the ugly barbed tip of the hook away, and then carefully slid the hook back through the seal's flipper. When the hook left him, the seal barked in pain, flinching away, rolling onto Brighid's foot, throwing her to the wet sand, her ankle twisted.

Immediately, he rolled away, flipper waving, whiskers twitching, barking in a low growl.

"Oh it's fine. I'm fine," she said, pulling herself to her feet and brushing her shins and thighs clean of the sand. "A little twinge, is all."

Urrrrr-ur…ur-ur-ur. The seal flapped his flipper, and lurched toward her.

He was bleeding profusely, she saw. She crouched and let him wiggle closer to her side. "That's it, a little closer. You need to have that patched up or you'll be a meal for someone else, with more teeth than you have, and we wouldn't want that, would we? No, indeed."

She had a moment of self-consciousness, realizing she was talking to a seal as if expecting him to understand her and respond, but…it felt as if he could. And it wasn't like she had anyone else to speak to, anyway, was it? Nor was there anyone to see or hear her folly.

She scooped a generous palmful of her homemade healing salve and gingerly spread it over the jagged hole in the seal's injured flipper, topside and bottom, and then wrapped the strip of cloth around several times, tying it tight.

"There. It's the best I can do, as I'm no nurse, nor a doctor for animals—a what would you call it? A veterinarian, isn't it?" She stroked his wet fur from the top of his head down his back, and he growled in his throat, a pleased sound, it seemed to her.

"If you want to thank me, bring me fish," Brighid said, standing up and backing away. "With my husband lost, I have no one to catch fish for me, and I'm dead tired of mutton."

Urrrrrr! Ur-ur-ur. Urrrk ur. Flopping backward a foot or two, the seal then wiggled around to face the sea, tail flapping, flippers slapping at the damp sand. Brighid watched, feeling an odd kinship to the seal. A sense of…recognition, even. Familiarity, perhaps, although that was the most foolish notion she'd ever had, and well Brighid knew it. Yet the feeling persisted, and she couldn't quite banish it.

Splashing into the water, the seal dove and shot away, then leapt and splashed down, and then poked his head out of the water, eyeing her from a distance of a dozen or so feet out. She waved, a hand lifted, her copper hair fluttering in the breeze. An eyeblink only, but when Brighid saw him again, she would have sworn instead of a seal, she saw a man, treading water, just his eyes above the surface, long black hair spread out on the waves like spilled ink. Those eyes, staring at her, they were limpid and dark and intelligent, and familiar. Another eyeblink, and there was a seal's tail spraying the sky with diamond-bright droplets, and then the sea was empty again.

Taking her empty pail, Brighid returned home,

built up her banked fire, and stirred the stew she'd made that morning.

That night, she dreamed again.

But not of Calum.

Of *him,* that man she'd seen the day prior. His lean, hard, powerful body. The long black hair, the taut muscles. She hadn't seen his face, but she knew he'd be as handsome as his body had been beautiful.

Not that it mattered. It was all conjecture. But where had the man come from? Where had he gone? He'd swum away and hadn't surfaced. A seal had, but…

Stories her mother had told around the fire when Brighid had been a little girl bubbled up from deep in her memory.

Selkies are real, Brighid, her mother had said, her dark eyes wide, firelight playing on her features. *Of that I'm absolutely sure. I've seen one. I came across a woman on the beach, and when she saw me, she dove into the water and swam away and only a seal appeared. I saw her again another time, too. They're real, Brighid. Don't you let anyone tell you any different. You find one, you find the skin of a selkie left behind when they change, they'll be trapped on the land and beholden to you for as long as you have it.*

She'd never really believed her mother's stories, though. Fireside tales, a mother entertaining her daughter during the long lonely evenings. Not real, not true.

But she'd seen it herself, a man vanishing into the

waves, and only a seal appearing out in the surf. Could it be real?

She woke restless, irritable. Hungry, and sick of mutton stew. Missing Calum. Hating the endless days alone, knowing Calum wouldn't be returning, knowing she had a life in front of her that would be the same as the years since Calum shipped out: Alone, herding goats and sheep, fixing fences, doing everything alone, making her way as best she could, one day at a time, until she grew too old to do it all.

She had fences to mend, sheep that needed shearing, wool that needed carding, and the garden needed weeding, but Brighid found herself instead wandering down between the dunes to the edge of the sea. It was another gray day, the sky heavy and leaden, the sea churning and wild and angry, petrichor thick in the air. Gulls surfed the wind currents, and sandpipers skittered toward the retreating waves, pecking at the slick wet sand and then darting away from the onrushing waves. Way out, far in the distance, a fluke tipped up out of the water and then dipped back down beneath the surly gray water, and then a plume spouted white skyward. The cry of the gulls was mournful, it seemed to Brighid, their harsh discordant caws striking her nerves. She wandered the shoreline, carrying her shoes, letting the bitter cold water lap at her feet.

Yet, even after she'd wandered nearly half a mile away from her section of the shoreline, the water remained empty, the shore barren. Eventually she had to return home and attend to chores. Yet as she hammered nails into a fence post and carded wool and yanked weeds, she continued to feel at loose ends, vaguely unsatisfied for reasons she couldn't pinpoint. She felt her loneliness more acutely than ever.

Again that night, she dreamed of the man she'd seen. Wondered what his name was, where home was for him, what his voice sounded like. What his hands would feel like on her skin. She dreamed he was in her home, crouched before the fire, a blanket around his shoulders. She dreamed of his eyes, dark as the night sky, intelligent and still somehow animal, watching her as she fluttered around the house, cooking, cleaning.

The next day, and the next, and every day for the following month, she wandered the shoreline just past dawn. She trapped lobsters, and thought of the seal who had knocked over her pail.

And then, when she'd begun to give up hope of seeing the man or the seal again, she wandered down to the shore in the minutes just before sundown, when the sun was just barely peeking up over the horizon, and the air was still warm but swiftly cooling and the light golden-scarlet and the wind gentle in her hair. And there he was, the seal. Breasted upon the sand, his tail flicking at the waves as they skirled around him. She knew it was him. Even if the strip of cloth hadn't still been tied around his flipper, she'd have known him. The preternatural way he stared at her with those limpid eyes. The way he remained still as she approached, just watching her, unafraid. Knowing, somehow. Welcoming, greeting.

Brighid knelt in the wet sand a few feet away from him. "Hello again. Are you well? How's your flipper doing?"

The seal flapped the flipper in question, splatting sand, barking.

She shuffled closer to him, reaching slowly and carefully. "I'm just going to slip this off you, now, okay?"

Another bark and a flap, tail slapping. He was massive, this seal. It hit her all over again as she crouched beside him. Huge, long, heavy, powerful. Those teeth, when he barked—they flashed white and sharp. Predator's teeth. He was still, however, as she unknotted the wet strip of cloth and tugged it off of him. He'd healed completely, with only a puckered scar remaining.

"There now, good as new." She shuffled back away from him, the makeshift bandage in hand.

Ur-ur-ur-ur.

"Oh, 'twas nothing. A bit of help for another of God's creatures. I still wouldn't mind if you brought me a fish or two, though."

Urk! Ur-ur.

He twisted around and carved under the waves, as graceful in the water as he was ungainly on land. She watched his dark form slice through water and vanish, and she found herself sitting in the sand, thinking of all the work that awaited her, and wishing she could dive into the ocean after him and swim with him beneath the waves and splash and catch fish and sun herself on a rock somewhere off shore.

She daydreamed, sea foam and icy water licking at her heels, the sun now past the horizon, the light hazy and red and golden.

Exhaustion snuck over her; the evening was warm now, and she wore a thick wool sweater of Calum's, and she was just so tired. She felt herself sinking down to the sand, pillowing her head on her arms, slipping into drowsy peacefulness as if in a dream, a return to girlhood when she could lie in the grass in the summer sun and let the warmth soak into her skin and bathe her closed eyes with a gentle yellow heat and drowse and feel time skip and hop and slip as she napped like a cat in a window.

There was movement. She was dreaming, though. Dreaming of Calum, returned. Scooping her up in his arms and carrying her to bed. Tucking a blanket around her shoulders. Watching her with large dark mysterious eyes.

Calum's eyes were gray, though, weren't they?

She fluttered her eyes, and saw craggy, swarthy features, a jaw like a cliffside, deep-set eyes like chips of blackest night, scars criss-crossing his cheeks, a thick black beard braided with strands of seaweed, long black hair around burly shoulders. Bare skin, a hint of a stomach, and then her eyes slid closed and when she opened them again, she was in her own bed and the house was empty.

Her door was open, though. Banging in the wind,

the light of a full moon shining bright on the wood planks, staining a line of wet footprints into silver pools.

"I'm dreaming. I must be dreaming." She rose from her bed, traipsed across the room to the nearest footprint.

There were grains of sand in the print. And her arms, her shoulders, her cheek were gritty with sand. It was in her hair. In her clothes. She followed the footprints outside into the night—there were flattened patches of grass, blades twitching upright still. It was a considerable distance to the next print, and the next, and then she was following impressions in the sand, where the edges of the impressions still slid in on themselves. Running, now, Brighid tripped and slid down the dune path to the sea and there he was, standing in the waves, hip-deep.

Watching her.

"Wait!" Brighid called, splashing knee-deep into the water toward him, uncaring that her skirt was getting soaked.

He hesitated, his posture that of a man about to dive into the water. He said nothing, waiting. She approached, the water at her thighs and then her belly, her clothing wet and sticking to her skin, the water icy cold. She was close enough that she could have touched him. The water did nothing, this close, to hide his manhood, although he was utterly unashamed of his nakedness.

Now that she was mere inches away, she had no idea what to say to him. She met his eyes, and he didn't look away, but his gaze was...alien. Animal. Other than human. An animal soul in a human body.

A momentary tableau, two pairs of eyes meeting, and then he twisted in a flash of dark skin and splashed into the sea, feet kicking the surface, and then he was gone. Brighid remained belly-deep in the frigid water, waiting, watching. Long minutes passed, and then, far, far, far out, a head surfaced. Too distant to make out anything but a vague shape, but she felt his gaze. And then another splash, a flash of a tail, and then the sea was just the sea, calm and tranquil once more.

Days passed, and Brighid continued to walk the shoreline in the mornings, and sometimes in the evenings as well.

One day she went to check her lobster traps, and her pail was gone.

The next day, it was back, sitting in front of her back door, full of fish. Cod, mackerel, tuna. Massive, fat, freshly caught.

The next morning, she left her pail on the sand near the rocks, where she'd first tended to the seal, where she'd first seen the naked man. By evening, it was gone; the next day, it was returned once more full of enormous fish.

For months, through the bitter winter and into spring, she would leave the pail on the beach in the morning and find it by her back door, full of fish, by evening. Those fish would sustain her for days, keep her fed, and prevent her from having to slaughter any more sheep.

And then, one night there was an awful storm, the kind where the wind blew so hard the windows rattled in their lead panes, and the thunder shook the foundations, and the rain clattered on the roof and walls and windows, and she could hear the sea roaring and churning. It blew angrily well past dawn, and then the sun rose and burned away the clouds, and trees had been downed across fences and sheep were missing and the goats were huddled together under a cluster of trees, bleating piteously.

It took Brighid hours to right everything, using Shem, her horse, to haul away the trees and then replace fence boards and find her sheep and herd the goats to a different pasture. It was evening before she found time to trudge exhaustedly down to the sea, which was still crashing loudly, whitecaps smashing onto the sand. Seaweed and driftwood littered the beach, enormous shells washed up from the depths, the corpse of something long dead water-bloated, bones showing through partially eaten flesh. Farther down, near the rocks, a dark shape.

Something alive, moaning low, writhing. A seal. *Her* seal, as she thought of him. She recognized his mottled coloring and the spray of whitish dots near his tail, and the scar on one flipper. He was injured again, this time grievously, a huge jagged spar of driftwood speared through his tail, high up, oozing blood.

As Brighid approached, the seal growled, wobbled toward her.

"I know, I know. I'm not sure I can fix that here. You need proper care, I think."

Another low rowling murmur, weak, piteous. Brighid knelt beside him, examining the injury. "This is bad, I'm afraid. It's not something I can just put salve and a bandage on." She moved toward his head, petting him carefully. "You know, I have a belief that you're a selkie. If you are, you could change, and I can help you to my house and care for you there."

Silence, and a profoundly intense stare from the seal, his eyes searching hers, looking for…she didn't know what, but she met his gaze steadily, not looking away.

And then he shimmied awkwardly, with difficulty and grunts of pain, into the water. Flapping, splashing, and disappearing beneath the waves. Not very far, not very deep; she could make out his form, but only a darker shape in the gray-green waves. There was…was it a flash of light, or her imagination? And then a roiling in the waves, and the dark shape slowly became lighter, thinner, smaller, legs flashing, kicking, an arm, long hair and that beard, and those eyes as he clawed back toward land, gasping, growling in pain. The spar was now lanced through his left thigh, high up, the jagged tip protruding out of the front of his thigh, the end dragging in the sand behind him. He was on his side, trying to keep the spar from dragging in the sand, clawing with both hands.

In one of his fists was…something dark, and

familiar. Fur? A hide, or a loose skin. Dripping wet, mottled and speckled. She crouched near him, propped her shoulder under his arm, and heaved him to his feet.

"It's not far," she said, "but you know the way, don't you, then?"

He didn't answer, just hobbled gingerly in the direction of her home. His injured leg dragged in the sand, and his weight pulled her down, slowed her, weakened her. She stiffened her spine and bore up under his massive weight. Calum was no small man, and she'd hauled him home drunk from the pub more than once before they'd moved to this farm on the coast, but the remembered weight of Calum seemed much, much less than this man. He just felt...dense, as if every pound of weight the seal carried, this man did as well. He was so heavily muscled as to defy belief, a massive, compact, hard, powerful man. And he was nearly limp, barely able to keep on his feet, even with her assistance.

They had to pause to breathe at the foot of the dunes, and Brighid looked back at their progress here and realized he'd left a trail of blood in the sand, a thick dark reddish-brown stain in the sand, blood sluicing down his thigh and off his foot and into the sand. After a few minutes of rest, Brighid worked herself to her feet, snugged her shoulder under his once more, and they painfully, slowly, laboriously dragged their way up the dune path. By the time they reached her back door, Brighid was sweating profusely and gasping for breath, every muscle screaming in protest.

He was barely conscious, now, deadweight crushing her into the ground. The spar—a hunk of wood cast off from some long ago shipwreck—was easily three feet in length and nearly a foot thick. It was smooth from being tossed in the briny waves for so long, but the pointed tip was jagged and razor-sharp. She got him inside, and to her bed, where he collapsed, his breath a pained whistle, groans emerging from his lips every few moments. He was bleeding everywhere, lying on his side, facing the wall, away from the doorway, the spar trailing down to the floor.

"I have to pull this out of you and stop the bleeding before you die from blood loss," Brighid said. "I need a few things first, though."

She hung a cook pot full of water on the hook in the fireplace to boil, and then cut up an old bedsheet into strips and set them in the water to sterilize. She gathered all the rags she had, and another sheet, and brought all of this, along with the freshly boiled bandages, into the bedroom.

After examining the wound, she leaned close to the man's ear. "I'm going to pull this out now. It will hurt quite a lot, I'm afraid." She shoved an old leather belt of Calum's between his teeth. "Bite down, and do not be afraid to scream. There's no one to hear but me."

Gritting her own teeth, Brighid took hold of the spar at the back of his thigh, a handful of rags close by. She braced her hand on his buttock, sucked in a steadying breath. "Ready? On three, then. One—two—*three*."

On the last count, she drew the spar out swiftly but carefully, and he screamed, an animal roar of agony as blood squirted out of the wound. He stiffened, and his hand clawed around his thigh, his fingers trembling. She gingerly moved his hand away and wadded a rag against the hole in the back of his thigh, and then another against the front side wound, and then swiftly wound a strip of bandage around the rags to bind them in place, tying it so tightly he snarled in protest.

"I'm sorry, I'm so sorry," she murmured to him, crooning. "It's got to be tight to slow the blood flow."

He was groaning and growling and snarling, the sounds utterly inhuman, totally animal. When the bandages were tied, she settled a blanket over him, as much to hide his nakedness as to keep him warm—although he was now shivering and shaking. He moaned low, a guttural sound, weak, pained.

Brighid left the rags on the bed and tossed the bloodstained hunk of wood outside, and then sank down into the grass, cross-legged, exhausted, breathing raggedly, night having fallen to bathe everything in darkness. Allowing herself to rest only for a few moments, Brighid forced herself back to her feet and inside, to check on her patient. He was asleep on the very edge of the bed, his back to the room, the blanket draped over his mammoth form. Her heart caught; a man hadn't been in her bed in over two years, nearly two and half years now and the sight put her heart in her throat and fear in her belly.

Calum she'd known. She'd grown up with him, born and raised in the same village, courted and married in that village and then moved to Dublin together, and then here. Calum had been familiar. Marrying him, going to bed with him had been…home from the very beginning.

This man, this nameless selkie, this creature from the ocean, part beast, part human…he was utterly unfamiliar.

Brighid was beyond exhaustion, having put in a full day's brutal work before finding him on the beach. Now she was…just done in, completely. And there was only the one bed, nowhere else to sleep save the grass outside or the hard floor.

Cursing under her breath, Brighid resigned herself to sharing the bed, because she desperately needed the rest. Her dress was sodden, however. She dug a nightgown out, checked to see if he was sleeping, and then quickly stripped out of her wet clothes, down to skin. She felt a shudder run down her spine as she tugged the nightgown on, and when she emerged from the neck hole, discovered that he was awake now, and watching her carefully, the fur clutched in both hands now, like a child with a favorite blanket.

"What am I going to do with you?" She asked, meaning it rhetorically. "You probably don't even think of nakedness as anything much, though, do you? You're certainly unbothered by it."

He didn't answer, only stared at her, and his eyes roamed her form, flicking from head to toe several times, scrutinizing her openly. He'd seen her before the gown was on, she was sure.

"I have to sleep," she said. "I can't very well kick you out now, but I also can't manage sleeping on the floor either. So I'm sharing. Do you understand me?"

Another long, curious, blank stare.

Brighid sat on the edge of the bed opposite him, meeting his gaze. "Do you speak English? Do you speak at all? Do you understand what I'm saying to you?"

He nodded, once.

Brighid laughed. "Well hell, man, I asked you three different questions, and I get a single nod in response?"

The intense, piercing, animal stare once more.

"Well, you nodded, so you understand English just fine, clearly. Can you speak though, or no?"

A long stare, and Brighid thought she was going to get more silence.

"I…speak." His voice was hoarse, gravelly, rough from extreme disuse. "Not well."

"Sounds fine to me." She slid a little further onto the bed. "What's your name?"

Another of those silent, intense stares that seemed to be a primary form of communication for him.

"Your name?" She touched her chest. "I'm Brighid."

He only shrugged, and shook his head.

"You don't have a name?"

He glanced at the ceiling briefly, a gesture of thought; he made a hoarse two-tone barking noise in his throat, and then shrugged again.

"Your name is…that noise?"

He shrugged, and then nodded again.

"Well, that's not going to work. I can't make that noise now can I?" She thought for a while, tapping her chin with a forefinger; all the while he stared at her, unblinking, a steady, intense gaze that no human could sustain. "How about Murtagh? Means skilled in the ways of the sea, which I feel is somewhat…erm, appropriate, given who or, um, what you are."

This got her the tiniest of smiles, a ghost of a smile at the corners of his mouth.

"Right. Well. I'm going to lay down, and you're going to stay there on that side, and you're going to keep your hands and your feet and your—" she glanced downward, an embarrassed suggestion, "—everything else, to yourself, you understand, Murtagh?"

"Yes." He murmured the word, a single syllable that felt heavy, thick, deliberate.

His voice wasn't accented in any way that she recognized, but merely as if words at all were a foreign concept to him.

She laid down then, under the blankets, whereas he was on top of them with a different blanket covering him. Layers between them. And still, she didn't fall asleep for a very long time, feeling him beside her, sensing him, smelling him. He smelled of man and of the sea, brine and musk. His breathing was steady but not sleep-slow, and she felt his stare.

"You're staring at me, Murtagh." She didn't look at him.

"Yes."

"Why?"

A silence. And then: "You…save me." Another silence. "You appear much good."

Brighid laughed. "I'm not sure what the means."

He was silent awhile, again. "To look upon you. It is good."

Brighid felt heat burn in her cheeks, and her pulse flutter. "Oh. I…thank you."

"Yes."

"Have you seen many women? Have you ever spoken to a woman? Like this?"

He grunted, a noncommittal or unsure sound. "Not as this. I see them. They swim from land, and I see them. Some with the coverings, and other times without the coverings. I like to see them better without the coverings. More of the skin. The body. It is good."

"I suppose you would." Brighid laughed. "Still a man, I see."

"Always am I man."

"Are you…a man, or a seal, or both?"

Another grunt. "This, that, all. I do not know. I am in the sea, the sea is in me. Her voice, her salt, her magic. She is everything."

"Have you ever been…" Brighid paused, realizing her question might be rude. But then, he wasn't human in the sense of understanding social mores, was he? "…with a woman?"

"To mate?" There was a hint of a smile. "Yes. She

does not know I am this. A selkie, as you call me. Only that I am a man, coming from the sea, and she likes to look upon me, and touch me, and we...do this. In the sea. I show her my way. The currents, the waves, my breath. Not like upon the land. Not very good, like that."

"Isn't it cold?"

"Not with me."

"I—she couldn't hold her breath as long as you can."

"I swim deep, very deep. To swim so deep, I do not breathe for a long, long time. As man, as seal—it is the same. I breathe for her." He paused. "For you."

He'd caught her slip up, then.

"She never knew you were a selkie?"

"No. She teach me this words. To speak as you. Before, I only—" he growled and barked, exactly like a seal, as if the sounds still lived inside him. "As this."

"So it was something you did, with her, over time?"

"She live as you, near the sea. She see me, we do the mating. I come back, swim to shore as a man. Many times. Until she does not come down to the sea again."

Brighid shivered. "How old are you?"

He was silent, and she realized he didn't know what this meant.

"How many seasons have you lived?"

"I swim to the winter hunting sea...many times. Too many for the counting. More than the changeless ones. Many, many more. The sea, she lives in me, and

I live in her. Long time. Long, long, long time. Before you, after you."

A vague answer that somehow left her feeling as if he was possibly ancient. His presence felt...*old*.

"Your man. He who lived here with you, before."

Brighid's heart caught. "Yes?"

"You wait for him." It was a question, but not a question. "To return to you from the far place."

"I—I don't know."

"No more waiting. He sinks down to the deepness, and he does not rise up again. No more breath."

"You know this?"

"The sea, she whispers her secrets, if you can hear her voice."

"I don't know what that means."

"Your words, this human speaking. It does not speak all the trueness of the sea, of the living of her, the feeling inside her. You do not know, for you are not of her, as I am."

Frustration boiled through her, because it felt like he was sharing something monumental, but she couldn't understand his convoluted usage of language. "I'm sorry, Murtagh, but I'm not following you."

"Follow? I am here."

"No, I mean...I don't understand what you mean."

"Oh. I mean—" he exhaled sharply, as if frustrated himself. "I ask the sea, and she tells me. I see you much with him, your man, and then he leaves on this shell upon the sea, and you are much alone. Much sad. Waiting for him to come back in his shell upon the sea. He will not. The sea knows him, now. She has swallowed him. He joins the many who breathe only the darkness of the deeps, now."

"He's dead, you mean."

"Dead is not living, not breathing?"

"Yes."

"Then he is dead."

A sob ripped out of her, the first she'd allowed herself since he'd left. Until that moment, she had refused to weep for him, to mourn him, for fear that to mourn him too soon would somehow mean she was being unfaithful to him. Giving up too soon.

But then...how did she know Murtagh was telling the truth? How could she believe him? He was a stranger from the sea, a real live selkie, if what she'd seen could be believed. Yet...if she believed he was a selkie—which the evidence of her eyes demanded—then it wasn't so great a stretch to believe that he could somehow communicate with the sea herself, that he might somehow have inside knowledge, so to speak, of Calum's death.

Tears were dripping down her cheek. She could still just barely make out Murtagh's form in the darkness, the shape of him dimly lit by the starlight from the window behind her. Murtagh reached out a hand, extending a thumb toward her cheek. She shied away, but then allowed him to smear her tear onto the pad of his thumb. Another tear slid down her cheek, and his thumb traced its path. Another tear fell, and his thumb pressed delicately against her tear duct.

And then he pressed his thumb to his lips, tasting her tears. "You make the sea from your eyes."

She sniffled. "It's called crying."

"Crying. Why do you do the crying?"

"It means I'm sad. For Calum. My man. My husband."

"Husband?"

"Mate…my mate."

Silence, and the shine and shimmer of his eyes fixed on her. "You are crying because you are sad your mate is dead."

"Yes."

"I felt sadness when this woman no longer came down to the sea to mate with me. I felt much pleased when she came down to the sea."

"We…Calum and I were mated for life."

"Always him, only him?"

Brighid nodded against the pillow. "Yes. Always him, only him."

"And now he is dead. Will you choose a new mate?"

"I…don't know."

"I could be your mate. Not for always, but for some of the seasons. I must swim to the winter hunting seas, but when I return with the warm currents, I will be your mate again."

Brighid laughed. "Such a male. No, Murtagh.

That's not how human mates work." She frowned. "Well, not for me. For some, it is."

"My hurt is strong. No more of this talking."

Brighid let out a slow breath, and turned away to face the window, watching gray-white shreds of cloud skirl across the moon, obscuring and then revealing, occluding stars here and there. Behind her, she heard Murtagh's breathing even out and slow, and she knew he was asleep.

Soon, so was she.

When she awoke, he was watching her.

He watched her as she prepared breakfast, and he watched her as she changed into a clean dress, and he watched her as she changed his dressing.

He watched her, and watched her, and watched her. She went about her chores, and he rested. She helped him to the outhouse, which he found detestable. She read to him from a book, which he found fascinating. When she stirred the fire to life in the fireplace, he was fearful but fascinated, his animal instinct warring with his human nature.

Another day passed thus, and another. He healed faster than a normal man might, Brighid reckoned. He was still unable to be on his feet for more than a couple of seconds, but that was more than she'd have expected for anyone else after so short a time.

A few days became a week, and a week became a month, and then two. His command of the structure of English never really improved, but he learned new words all the time, and he became ever more articulate.

At no point did he ever let go of the fur pelt; it was always, always clutched in one hand, or tucked under his arm, cradled against his ribcage. He was fiercely protective of it.

One night, as they lay in bed, him above and she under the covers, Brighid found herself staring at the pelt curiously. She reached out a hand, tentative and cautious; Murtagh's warning snarl was pure animal.

"I'm sorry. I'm just curious." She withdrew her hand, watching him.

He tucked the fur deeper underneath him, out of sight. "It is not for you."

"I know." She kept her distance, but let the question she'd been harboring bubble out. "The legends about selkies…they say if you don't have your pelt, you can't change back, that you won't be able to return to the sea."

He snarled again. "*Not* a *pelt*. That is the skin your human hunters take from my changeless brothers. This—" he clutched the fur tightly, squeezing it in gesture. "It is…it is *me*."

"I'm sorry. I won't touch it, I'm just…I'm curious, I guess."

"What you say is true. Without it, I am only a man, and I cannot speak to the sea, and she cannot speak to me. I can hear her, but I cannot speak to her. She speaks, but I hear only the waves, not her voice. If I do not speak to her, I cannot change back, and I will be like your man, but on land. What is your word for sinking under the waves?"

"Drowning."

"Drowning. I will drowning here on the land. Already, the beast craves the sea. The drowning is soon. I must touch the water, see her, feel her. Hear her."

"You can still barely move, Murtagh. I don't know how it works when you change back, but you're not healed enough yet to swim. You'd barely make it down to the water as you are now."

He rumbled, a seal's growl of unhappiness. "I cannot change back yet. But I must touch the sea." There was a pained note of desperation in his deep, guttural voice. "I *must*. She calls me."

Brighid fashioned a crude crutch, the next day. Wrapped his leg tightly, and tried to convince him to don a pair of Calum's old trousers, but Murtagh refused.

"I am not a man, to wear a man's clothing."

It was growing ever more difficult for Brighid, having him around naked all the time. She found her gaze wandering to him throughout the day, whether he was covered by the blanket or not. And now, upright, her shoulder under his arm, her crude crutch under his other, assisting him slowly down toward the beach, his skin was warm against her, smooth and firm. His manhood swung between his legs, and she tried to not stare, but the battle was a losing one, for her.

If he noticed her gaze, or felt it, he gave no indication.

When they finally, after a long, exhausting trek,

reached the water's edge, Murtagh tossed the crutch aside, gingerly unwrapped the dressing and handed the bundle of cloth to Brighid, and then hopped on one leg into the waves, and then when he was too deep to hop any longer, he sat down in the water and used his hands to push himself deeper, until the waves lapped at his throat and chin.

She was grateful to be away from him, because his proximity, the feel of his muscles and his flesh created a dark, dangerous fluttering in her belly, made her thighs clench and her breasts ache, in a way she hadn't felt in so, so long. It felt like a betrayal to Calum to feel such things, and she attempted to push it away. Yet the longer Murtagh remained in her home, the longer he slept in her bed—even separated by layers of blankets, and even though he had made no move to touch her in any way—the harder it became to ignore the feelings.

"Come." Murtagh's voice called out to her. "Come feel the sea with me."

It was a warm day, the sun bright, the sky clear blue, the wind a gentle breeze. She let out a breath, gathered her skirts up around her knees, and waded in to her calves.

Murtagh watched, and frowned. "No. You cannot feel her with the clothing over your skin. You cannot breathe her breath, you cannot feel her."

"I'm not taking off my clothes in front of you, Murtagh."

"Why?"

She had no answer for that. Modesty was not an idea he would understand. She'd tried, and he'd only given her the blank, uncomprehending stare.

"Just...because."

Murtagh stared. "You fear me." His lifted his head, his nostrils flaring. "I smell your fear."

"I'm not afraid of you, Murtagh."

"Your words do not agree with the scent of fear." He remained where he was, watching her. "What do you fear?"

"It's not fear, exactly."

"I do not understand, then. I smell fear."

"It's hard to explain."

He shook his head. "She said that. When she did not wish for me to understand."

"What wouldn't she want you to understand?"

"Why she couldn't come with me, out into the deeps. Down deep, away, to the winter hunting sea. I could breathe for her. I could teach her to hear the sea. But she would not, and I did not understand why. She only would tell me that it was hard to explain."

"Some things *are* hard to explain, Murtagh."

"No. You do not *want* to. This is not the same as *cannot*. Not as I am understanding your words to mean."

He was cunning. She couldn't argue with his logic. "Fine. I don't want to explain some things to you."

"Why?"

"Because it is painful and confusing. Because I don't understand them myself."

"Try."

"I'm not afraid of you, not like a…like prey fears the predator. You are a man, and I am a woman. I had a husband, a mate. Now I don't, and I'm lonely."

"I am here. You are not lonely anymore."

She laughed. "I suppose that's true."

"I am a *male*, not a *man*." He lifted the fur. "I am this." He tapped his chest. "And this. I am both."

"It's just…you say the sea told you Calum is dead."

"Yes."

"I can't just…forget him."

Murtagh sighed, and lay back in the waves so he was submerged completely and then rose up again, a peaceful, contented expression on his rugged features, water sluicing down from his beard, his hair pasted to his shoulders. "No forgetting. I do not forget her, the woman from beyond the dunes. Never, never will I forget her. She was sad, and much alone, and her body was not strong. I think she became dead, and so no longer came down the sea to mate with me. This is sad, inside me, that she is dead. But I do not forget. Also I do not cease to be alive. She has become dead, not me. Must I remember her and only her, for always? What if I choose also to remember you?" He gazed at her steadily, and his dark, sharp predator eyes were fierce and intense and wise. "Remember your man, your Calum. But also be alive. Breathe the sea. Breathe your land. Touch the wind. Touch the sea. Feel the life in all things."

"Murtagh—"

He did not look away, did not stop to hear her protest. "Feel the life in me. I am here. I am alive. I am a male, and a man, and I am here. He is not. He is in the deepness of the sea, breathing only darkness. I breathe life. Remember him, but also be alive."

"What if it's not that simple for me?"

"Life is life. It flows like the currents—always, always, always. A death does not slow the currents. We must swim, or the darkness will be our only breath."

Wisdom of the wild. Simple, practical.

She'd mourned and waited for three years. She knew in her heart and soul that Murtagh was telling the truth, that Calum was gone. So why could she not…be alive?

Slowly, hesitantly, Brighid reached up and unbuttoned her dress, baring more and more flesh with each button undone. Murtagh's gaze was steady and as mysterious as ever, unreadable. When the buttons were all undone, she lifted the garment off and set it with Murtagh's dressings, the whole weighed down by the crutch. And then she was naked, standing in the breeze and the sunlight, with Murtagh's gaze openly perusing her.

She waded deeper, and even on such a warm day the water was icy cold, making her bones ache. Deeper and deeper…closer and closer to Murtagh. Who watched, never looking away, not moving a single muscle as she waded up to her thighs. And then she was standing beside him, the water at her thighs, all of her bared. He'd watched her change more than once, despite her attempts to change when he wasn't watching, but this was different. There was no privacy in that small home, being only one room. Here, it was the open sea, the beach, the sunlight, and her own choice to strip naked so he could look at her.

"Go under. Feel her." Murtagh's voice was low, the words nearly inaudible.

Brighid waded deeper, and then, with a deep sharp breath, dove under, feeling the icy waves close around her, and she heard then only the silent roar of the undersea world, muted and muffled and so loud, somehow. He was there. Beside her. Toeing off the seafloor with one foot, the other leg trailing behind, his hands pulling at the water.

He reached out, and took her hand. His eyes were wide and round and not quite human, so dark, a seal's eyes in a man's face. "Listen."

"For what?"

He shook his head. "Not *hear*, as to hear the birds or the waves or my words." He tapped her chest, a brief but heart-palpitating contact of his finger just above her breasts. "Listen."

She held onto his hand and closed her eyes, and tried to listen, but she only heard the waves, the gulls. She felt him, though. So close. His hip touched hers, and his hand was huge and strong. She heard him, felt him. Only him.

"Do you hear her?" He asked, after a while.

She opened her eyes and met his gaze. Shook her head. "No. All I hear is you."

"I was silent."

"No..." She tapped his chest as he had hers. "All I heard was you."

A ghost of a smile, then. He drifted closer. She could just barely touch the seafloor with her toes, enough to keep her chin above the waves, which sometimes lapped against her nose and mouth so the taste of the sea was on her lips. And then all she could taste was him, his mouth, the brine on his lips and the heat of his breath, and his hands were closing around her, carving a hot wild path from her shoulder blades to the small of her back and paused there, as if to give her time to absorb the reality of his touch. She couldn't breathe and didn't want to, because this was like coming alive all at once, after so long being...something in between alive and dead.

God, the ache. Her thighs quaked and clenched and she nuzzled closer, deepening the kiss, telling him with her body and her mouth and her hands burying in his beard that this was okay, more than okay, that she needed it. And then his hands slid down to cradle her buttocks, and she was gripping his arms and his shoulders and tracing the mighty muscles of his back and clutching his backside and she felt him nudging against her, his manhood pressing hot and hard against her womanhood.

Brighid gasped at the feel of him, whimpered.

Murtagh broke the kiss. "Breathe me. Trust in me."

"What?"

He swelled his lungs to capacity, blew the breath out and sucked in an even greater inhalation, and then locked his mouth against hers and tumbled them backward together under the waves. Fully immersed, the cold burned, and then she felt nothing but Murtagh, his hands scouring her skin and his tongue on her teeth and his legs propelling them powerfully out into the currents. Where was his hide? His hands were all over her, so he wasn't clutching it. Had he set it aside? Hidden it? She didn't know, and the ability to think about it eroded as his kiss pressed breath into her lungs, as his hands ignited fiery desire inside her. Even injured he could swim with strength and grace and power that was very truly inhuman; he was carrying them together out into the depths, twisting them together beneath the waves, farther and farther from shore.

Brighid clung to him and kissed him back and kicked her legs with his. The waves rolled above them and Murtagh's powerful strokes carried them effortlessly. And then he was pressing against her entrance, and she moaned into his mouth and took him within her, and then she could hear the sea.

Her song was deep and sorrowful and wild and joyful and exuberant and melancholy, a complex and multilayered creation of the many miles and leagues which makes up the sea, from the shores of Africa to

China, from America to Ireland, and everything in between, as Murtagh moved with her, breathing for her, breathing through her, as his hands and lips and manhood fused with her skin and her mouth and private aching heat, she heard the sea in his movements, she heard the sea in his voice. He was the sea, a creature of her, in her, from her. A being coalesced of pure oceanic power, distilled essence of the brine.

Brighid wept at the voice of the sea. Her words were in a language Brighid did not know but somehow still understood, but as if hearing Gaelic spoken by a Scot, or through a translator. Unclear, but recognizable. The sea was inside Brighid, in her soul, in her blood, in her brain. In her bones and muscles and sliding through her most tender flesh. The sea was loving her.

As their bodies merged and collided and slid and moved, Murtagh took them deeper and deeper until pressure weighed upon her ears and eyes and bones, and he twisted and rose up once more, gliding through the water with Brighid clutched in his arms, swimming with her in a graceful ballet, a mating dance at once animal and human.

Breathe me feel me touch me hear me

That was the song of the sea.

Swim play eat drink live love laugh cry dive drown breathe breathe breathe me know me

The sea whispered to her. Sang to her. The crash of surf on a distant shore was the melody, the rolling waves in the far wild depths was the rhythm, the tides a counterpoint, the song of the whales and dolphins and the chatter of seals and otters and the cry of gulls and albatross and the shimmering flash of schools of fish, these were the chorus. And Brighid heard it all. She could sing this song; her voice longed to join in, her body knew the dance, her soul knew the ageless tune.

And then they broke the surface and the sand was under her feet and the surf was crashing around them and their joining was lost, and the song was lost.

Murtagh was gasping for breath and his man/seal inky black eyes were fierce and intense. "Did you hear her?"

She couldn't speak. Only nod, whimpering. "Yes," she managed to choke out the word. "I heard, Murtagh. I heard her."

His smile was predatory and playful and happy. "You heard. The sea, she speaks to you. This is good."

And so it began.

As he grew in strength, he helped her with chores, and they made their way down to the sea and swam and joined together and Brighid listened eagerly to the song of the sea, which she could only hear when tumbling in the waves with Murtagh inside her.

Days, weeks, months...and then Murtagh was as healed as he was going to be, a limp forever in his step, but his strokes under the sea were as effortless and powerful as ever.

And then, one day, Murtagh was out checking lobster traps, and Brighid was cleaning her little home. And she found, tucked inside an old pot that had been shoved behind the stove, Murtagh's sealskin.

It was silky, still damp, somehow. Thick, soft, and velvety. She didn't remove it from the pot, only stroked it gently.

A thought occurred to her. She could hide it again, and Murtagh would stay with her.

She felt him needing the sea. Needing his freedom. He was restless. He would wake in the middle of the night and stand on the dune, staring out at the moon on the sea.

Her hand in the pot, fingers buried in the fur, Brighid heard a step behind her.

Murtagh's eyes were wild and angry and fearful. He was utterly still, tensed. "Brighid." His voice was a deep, dark rumble. "That is mine."

"I know, Murtagh. I found it by accident." She didn't want him to leave. She didn't want to lose the song of the sea, or the way he felt, the beauty of their song together beneath the waves.

"Would you hide it from me?" He took a step toward her. "Trap me here on this shore, with you?"

She shook her head, feeling a tear trickle down her cheek. "No, Murtagh." She forced herself to stand up, to turn away, showing him her empty hands. "No. I wouldn't ever do that."

Brighid left the house, and walked down the path

with the dune grass tickling her calves and the sand skritching underfoot and the breeze in her hair and the sea in her nostrils and the gulls overhead.

He was going to leave.

She felt it.

His step was silent on the sand, but she sensed him behind her. "She calls me. Cries out to me."

"I know."

"Swim with me."

She held back a sob. "No, Murtagh. I can't handle that kind of goodbye."

"I meant…swim away." He pointed, away out to sea, south. "Far. Down deep, to the winter shores."

"I can't."

"I can breathe for you, Brighid."

She shook her head. "No, Murtagh, it's not that. I know you can. But…you belong out there. I belong here."

"Our song together is beautiful music."

"It is."

"I would sing that song with you for always."

"I cannot live in the sea, and you cannot live on the shore."

He breathed into her hair. "Never before have I cursed my nature. Now I do."

"No, Murtagh. Your nature is…beautiful. You are of the sea, and she is of you."

"You are of me, and I am of you."

She shook her head again. "It can't work."

He growled, an animal sound of displeasure. "I will return, then. When the summer currents call us back, I will return here. This will be my summer shore. You will come down to the sea, and we will swim together and sing the song of the sea."

She nodded, her breath catching. "Okay."

He strode past her, his sealskin clutched in one hand. Waded into the waves, naked, as the first time she saw him. As he always was. Nude and beautiful, masculine perfection. Deeper, until he was waist deep, and then he paused and turned around. Stared at her, and now she saw a world of emotion and intelligence and personality in that animal stare. No goodbye, no one last kiss, no sentiment. Just that silent stare, and then he dove into the waves and there was a gentle flash of greenish light under the waves and the surface roiled, and then the pale form of his naked body darkened and then there was only a seal, twisting in the waves, head poking up over the surface, dark eyes staring at her. And then another a splash and a flip of his tail and he was gone, streaking away out into the sea.

Brighid let herself sob, then.

But only for a little while.

The surf lapped at her feet, as if to comfort her, and perhaps it was her imagination, but the icy water didn't make her bones ache like it used to. She waded a little deeper, hiking her skirts up around her waist, and she felt the tug of the currents. A split-second decision had her stripping the dress off and diving naked into the water and she felt the sea around her, heard, perhaps, a distant note of a song, as of the strains of a violin from a window across the city.

She swam, and the sea welcomed her.

Her tears mingled with salt of the brine.

She could almost hear his voice, the bark and growl of a seal joining his brothers and sisters on a long southward journey.

Eventually the shore called out to her, the bleat of goats and sheep, the waving grasses and the warmth of the sun and the crimson glow of sunset on the horizon and the crackle of a fire on a cold winter night.

He would return. The tides would bring him to her, and she would swim with him. And until then, she could dive down beneath the waves and hear his voice in the song of the sea.

Where The Heart Is: Where Are You, Lover?

you can't always get what you want
so the song goes
I wanna be in love,
know what every other lover knows
someone to hold me, someone to kiss
someone to fight with, someone to miss

Been down a thousand roads
played a thousand chords
sang a thousand songs
about a thousand wrongs
sang about men always leaving
men I'll never love, and how I leave 'em
so many words, so many lines
one-night stands, too many times
get up on stage, there's only one mic
sing my songs, only my voice
play my guitar, only my chords
only my strings, only my words

you can't always get what you want
so the song goes
I wanna be in love,
know what every other lover knows

someone to hold me, someone to kiss
someone to fight with, someone to miss

hello life, are you listenin'
I've got one request
one thing I want, and screw the rest
can I get another mic next to mine
someone to write the next line
can I get another voice, singing harmony
sound check, mic check, play guitar with me
long days, long roads, drive with me
late nights and shit gigs, another set with me

you can't always get what you want
so the song goes
I wanna be in love,
know what every other lover knows
someone to hold me, someone to kiss
someone to fight with, someone to miss

where are you, lover
can you hear me
come closer, baby, wanna feel you near me
this bed is too big without you
life is too short, can't live without you
where are you, lover
I'm begging
don't stay gone, don't be long
I'm writing this song, and maybe I'm wrong

but what we had, baby,
maybe it's meant to be
maybe you are meant for me
maybe this love isn't just fiction
I want you I need you, my fingers are itching
need to touch you need to feel you

so don't stay gone, don't be long
I'm writing this song, and maybe I'm wrong
but what we had baby,
maybe it's meant to be

I know what they say
can't always get it your way
you can't always get what you want
so the song goes
I wanna be in love,
know what every other lover knows
someone to hold me, someone to kiss
someone to fight with, someone to miss

hello life, are you listenin
I've got one request
one thing I want, and screw the rest
can I get another mic next to mine
someone to write the next line
can I get another voice, singing harmony
sound check, mic check, play guitar with me
long days, long roads, drive with me
late nights and shit gigs, another set with me

Where The Heart Is: Tall Dark & Handsome

hey mister tall dark and handsome
your smile took me for ransom
let's meet on the floor and get to dancin'
don't have to be fancy
forget about tomorrow, it don't mean a thing
i'll give you a wink, you'll buy me a drink
kiss me in the hall
push me up against the wall

hey mister tall dark and handsome
you got this heart of mine, it's for ransom
you took it when you danced with me
let me think you fancied me
you kissed me in the hall
and loved me up against the wall
you carried me across the floor
and then showed me the door

hey mister tall dark and handsome
you took me for ransom
when you bought me another one
and said it's just a little fun
you didn't ask for my number

and i gotta wonder
if this is just for tonight
then why does it feel so right

Hey mister tall dark and handsome
here's your ransom
keep it, I don't need it
here's my heart, just don't bleed it
I'll give you a wink and you'll buy me a drink
and show me the back seat of your car
if we even make it that far

I wish i could say I'm not usually like this
bought with a drink and a kiss
but baby that'd be a lie
so don't be shy and don't ask why
that's a song for another night
so play your cards right
mister tall dark and handsome
take me for ransom
just gimme a wink and buy me a drink

Where The Heart Is: Cry All Night

dawn breaks, pink on the beach
lovesick, you're out of reach
you sat in the shadows, listening
you missed my tears, didn't see 'em glistening
I cried that night
yeah, i cried all right

You said it won't work
I said it won't hurt
that was me lyin',
because baby we shoulda kept tryin'
instead you walked away, sighin'
and now i'm alone and i'm dyin'

dawn breaks, pink on the street
lovesick, can't even eat
all night I think of you
all night I dream of you
stay up all night, whisper your name
stare at the ceiling, left wondering
if you feel the same
and I cry at night
god, I cry all right

You said it won't work
I said it won't hurt
that was me lyin',
because baby we shoulda kept tryin'
instead you walked away, sighin
and now i'm alone and I'm dyin

Where The Heart Is: When Your Heart's Gone

you walked into my life,
with your dark skin and deep eyes
I tried to resist you, tried not to kiss you
you speak soft and you talk slow
you've got strong hands and few words
but I hear it anyway, everything you don't say
I tried to resist you, tried not to kiss you
but god, your lips,
the way you moved your hips
the way you said my name
and said you felt the same
the way you took my hand
and kissed me in the sand

you said it won't work
i said it won't hurt
you said it's just for the moment, let's own it
what I didn't say was,
here's my heart just break it
what I didn't say was, I'm feeling love,
can't shake it
baby, that was me lyin',
because baby we shoulda kept tryin'

now I'm sitting here without you
wondering how do you go on
when your heart's gone
because you walked away, said you can't stay

it was all too much,
god, it was more than lust
my heart's full of rust, my soul's full of dust
it's such a rush, it's more than a crush
more than your strong hands and slow sighs
more than your soft words, and dark eyes
it's something I can't define
something in your eyes, god, they shine
makin me want, makin me wish
makin me moan, makin me kiss
makin me rush, makin me miss
everything about you

I couldn't resist you, tried not to kiss you
but god, your lips,
the way you moved your hips
the way you said my name
and said you felt the same
the way you took my hand
and kissed me in the sand

you said it won't work
i said it won't hurt
you said it's just for the moment, let's own it

what I didn't say was, here's my heart just break it
what I didn't say was, I'm feeling love, can't shake it
baby, that was me lyin',
because baby we shoulda kept tryin'
shoulda kept tryin'
now I'm sitting here without you
wondering how do you go on
when your heart's gone
because you walked away, said you can't stay

Where The Heart Is: Until It's Gone

don't cry, don't cry, don't cry
It won't take the hurt away
it won't wash the pain away
keep your chin up and just hold on
just keep breathing until it's gone

so what if he never loved you
who cares if he just used you
his kisses abused you
his beautiful body unglued you
his charm subdued you
and then he walked away,
and screwed you

don't cry, don't cry, don't cry
It won't take the hurt away
it won't wash the pain away
keep your chin up and just hold on
just keep breathing until it's gone

So what if you're all alone
i know, you're not made of stone
it's okay to be broken
take a moment, so what if it's stolen
these midnight tears won't mend you
this heartbreak won't end you

don't cry, don't cry, don't cry
It won't take the hurt away
it won't wash the pain away
keep your chin up and just hold on
just keep breathing until it's gone

Where The Heart Is:
Shouldn't Be In Love

shouldn't be in love, but baby I am
I know it's crazy, but I don't give a damn
god you're like a drug, I'm addicted
I want you, but I'm conflicted
shouldn't let myself have you,
but whenever I'm near you I come unglued
can't keep it in, can't stay subdued

shouldn't be in love, but baby I am
I know it's crazy, but I don't give a damn
shouldn't want you near me
but you're inside me, can you hear me
I'm praying you need me, baby say you do
I'm lying in bed, dreaming of you
cuz I remember you moving, gliding
can't get over you, baby I'm trying
why can't I have you,
does it have to be so complicated
the love and the need still haven't faded

shouldn't be in love, but baby I am
I know it's crazy, but I don't give a damn
I feel you inside me
don't mean it like that, but I wish it was true

truth is, baby, i need you
missing you and wishing you were here,
it's tried me
I hate each day without you,
when I should be happy
I'm getting what I wanted,
but you're not here and I'm dying
moving on shouldn't be so hard, but I'm trying
it's not working, my heart is hurting
getting over you, thought it'd be a sure thing

I shouldn't be in love, but baby I am
I know it's crazy, but I don't give a damn
loving you is crazy but baby I can't shake it
it's gonna get me hurt, but I can't fake it
so many days without, I can't take it
I shouldn't be in love, but I am
I know it's crazy, but I don't give a damn

Where The Heart Is: One In A Million

couldn't pick you out of a lineup
maybe I should put a sign up
on my heart says out of order, out of business
don't ask to stay,
baby that ain't what this is
come morning, baby, I'm gone
yeah i'll come over, won't stay long
If I gave you my number, boy,
you took it hooker sinker and line
because those digits on the napkin ain't mine

You're one in a million, boy
you're readin' me right,
this ain't a ploy
you can walk into my bed,
but not into my heart
my skin may be soft,
but my heart is what's hard
you're one in a million, boy
you're hearin' me right, ain't playin' coy
so take what i'm offering,
this body of mine
don't ask questions,
yeah I'll be just fine
because you're one in a million, boy

Where The Heart Is: Just Need Tonight

you got me like whiskey
so baby just kiss me
tip me back and drink me down
pick me up, off with my gown
I ain't no Cinderella, no fancy glass shoes
you ain't no Hollywood fella,
on a list of who's who
so just pay the tab
call us a cab
I've had a few drinks, can you taste 'em
don't have many hours, don't waste 'em
you got me like whiskey
all you gotta do is kiss me
tip me back and pour me down
hold me up, off with my gown

Don't need a pickup line
so don't ask me the time
I like whiskey, don't drink wine
don't need salt, don't need lime
This ain't a date,
so baby don't wait
don't mind the hangover,
won't ask to stay over
Don't need a promise, don't need a call

all I want is this, baby that's all
sweaty skin and whiskey lips
beat of your heart and hands on my hips
bodies in motion, shadows like oceans
touch like devotion, kiss like a potion
you got me riled, so baby be wild
no number to dial, just keep me a while

don't need tomorrow, just need tonight
I ain't no virgin, won't wear white
take me out and show me around
pick me up, show me the town
butter me up, I might go down
don't need my number, ain't a booty call
this ain't love, and I won't fall
all I want is you and me naked
take me to bed, I won't fake it
baby just get me screaming
and then leave me dreaming
Won't hear me weeping
This ain't love, I don't want keeping
here comes the sun
baby, sure was fun

Don't need a pickup line
so don't ask me the time
I like whiskey, don't drink wine
don't need salt, don't need lime
This ain't a date,

so baby don't wait
don't mind the hangover,
won't ask to stay over
Don't need a promise, don't need a call
all I want is this, baby that's all
sweaty skin and whiskey lips
beat of your heart and hands on my hips
bodies in motion, shadows like oceans
touch like devotion, kiss like a potion
you got me riled, so baby be wild
no number to dial, just keep me a while

Where The Heart Is: Faking This

If I take this moment, will there be any more?
If I let you go,
can I watch you walk out the door?
If I take this moment and own it,
it'll be the end us, won't it?
There's a million reasons why written in the sky
they gleam like the moon
they foretell of you leavin' me soon
a million reasons you can't stay
a million reasons you're walking away

If I just lie here in the dark
maybe I'll dream of you
if I pretend my hand is your hand,
maybe I'll scream for you
If I close my eyes and wish,
maybe I'll remember your kiss
but I'm not all right,
baby I'm faking this

This won't be the end of me
so baby don't pretend for me
but did you have to look back?
The kisses, the whispers, was it an act?
the way you held me

from night till the morning,
the way you took my heart without warning
were they just lines, was it a game?
I said it's all too much, and you felt the same,
Your touch is more than a memory,
your kiss, what it meant for me
your words, what they did to me
getting lost in the stars, it felt like a dream
you left and you're gone, was it what it seemed
did you love me, or were we just sex
do you love me, or am I an ex?

If I just lie here in the dark
maybe I'll dream of you
if I pretend my hand is your hand,
maybe I'll scream for you
If I close my eyes and wish,
maybe I can remember your kiss
But I'm not all right,
baby I'm faking this

Where The Heart Is: Don't Look At Me

Don't look at me, baby boy
I don't want you to know
don't want you to see
where it is I go

what I do
just to buy you that toy
I don't want you to know
I don't want you to know

I wait till you're asleep
and I kiss your cheek
tug the blankets up higher
tuck you in tighter
it's just another day, just another week
another night digging deep
another night wearing a whole lotta not so much
working that late night rush
dealing with the late night crush
bending over way too low
putting way too much on show
letting all the drunks see
way too much of me

don't look at me, baby boy
I don't want you to know

I don't want you to see
so don't look at me
I hope you never know
I hope you never see
where I go
what I do, baby boy
just to buy that toy
don't look at me
don't look at me
because I don't want you to know
baby, baby, baby, don't look at me
I don't want you to know
I don't want you to see

I do it all for you
you're all I've got
And I wanna give you everything
I know it ain't a lot
but it's all I can do
and I do it all for you
I do it all for you.

Where The Heart Is:
Another Bar, Another Mic

truck stop diner outside Miami
got my good jeans on, favorite cami
guitar in the front seat beside me
and another gig behind me
got a bad boy habit
an addiction I just can't beat
burns hotter than whiskey neat
wash my hands
but it don't wash the bad boy off me
so I slide on in, get another coffee
I always know it's gonna hurt
but that don't stop me
they do me wrong
so I put 'em in a song

Every night it's the same old thing
another bar, another mic
another hey pretty thing
lemme hear you sing
another hey little mama,
let's cut the drama
another town and one more gig

another beer and one more swig
another hotel bar and a good-lookin liar

I've got another gig tomorrow
another night to sing my sorrow
got my six-string Taylor in the seat beside me
the one boy won't kiss and tell
the one boy won't put me thru hell
I'm just a six-string singer
a first-light leaver
sneak out while you're sleepin'
creep out while you're dreamin'
love you hard and leave you reachin'
love you fast, and leave you weepin'

Every night it's the same old thing
another bar, another mic
another hey pretty thing
lemme hear you sing
another hey little mama,
let's cut the drama
another town and one more gig
another beer and one more swig
another hotel bar and a good-lookin liar

There's No Place like Home: From Christian's Journal

A gladness sparks in me,
A fragment of madness,
A particulate of joy.
It is a small thing, a tiny thing,
elemental, wild, tremulous, and fragile.
There is frost on my heart,
a crackling coldness at the edges,
spiderweb cracks reaching hungry fingers inward.

The spark, it warms me,
pushes at the edges of the ice.
Whence comes this gladness?
Whence, the mad fragment?
Whence, the fractal iota of joy?
I know not,
I know only that it judders and shakes
inside me,
singing a nearly silent song,
trembling in the shadows
of my soul.

Does it come from the cool breeze
on my skin,
which awakens some shiver of memory?

Does it come from the shiver of memory itself,
from the slither of knowing
coiled deep in my fallow, fertile mind?
If Memory slithers,
it is a silent, sneaking serpent,
Which craves to remain unfound.
But the slither, I feel it,
I feel the glide of scales,
feel the smooth skin in hints,
feel the questing hiss of the tongue.
Memory is a serpent,
And I seek it in the tall grasses,
watch the grass as it moves against the wind,
evidence of that which I seek.
Is it thence from which comes
the spark of gladness?
I think no.

Because it is a false joy.

Think of the madman,
clad in straitjacket and chains,
howling in his padded cell.
He laughs, does he not?
He ululates, and drools, and gibbers.
But through it all, he laughs.
A wild cackle.
A crazed guffaw.
A manic chortle.

Thus am I.
Minute by minute,
Hour by hour,
Day by day,
Week by week,
Month by month,
I sit in this be-damned imprisoning chair,
rickety, ancient, and creaking,
staring at the swaying palms,
suffering the heat,
batting at flies.
Scribbling.
Hoping my scribbles will form a net,
which will ensnare that wily serpent:
Memory.

I cast my net wide.
I weave it with strands of madness,
Threads of fiction,
Filaments of truth,
All part of the warp and weft of my tapestry,
Which is my net.
Which is all that I am,
all that I have of myself,
whatever sense of self I possess
in this mad, waiting time.

So,
This spark of gladness...

What is it?
It is momentary, at best.
Easily devoured by the cold,
Drowned in the shadows
Which obscure my mind.
I want to cup that spark in my hands,
frame it with my palms,
protect it, nurture it.
Breathe gently upon it,
catalyze the spark into a flame,
Fan the flame into a blaze,
Pour accelerant on the blaze,
Make it a pyre,
A wildfire,
An inferno,
Brighter than the sun,
hotter than an African noon,
So bright it sheds light upon me,
banishing the shadows,
Illuminating the serpent,
Which is named Memory.

I wish to be free of this place.
Rise from this wheeled chair
which is my prison,
Free from the plaster binding
my arms and my legs,
Free from the pain in my ribs,
Free from the throbbing emptiness

of my knowledge of self,
Free to venture forth,
And find

ME.

Find the ruins of the life I led,
And resurrect them.
Rebuild them.
Or, failing that,

Build anew.

There's No Place Like Home: From Christian's Journal

There is nothing but the Sea,
The scudding of the wind,
And the twisting melt of Time against my skin.
Nothing but the knowledge of our sin,
And my guilt,
oozing under my flesh like sludge.
Nothing but your dark truth,
coating the fine hairs on my arm like a mist.

Fever dreams in the darkness,
as I lie in the belly of a beast:
You, love, with your lips sewn shut,
each stitch written in ink-black threads,
The wounds where needle threaded flesh
raw and red and bleeding;
Me, staggering through venomous shadows,
alcohol seeping from my skin
like leaking poison;
A grave, the marble headstone gleaming
wet in a driving rain,
the mound of grass jeweled with raindrops—
Old, rotten flowers going gray,
forgotten 'neath the stone—

five letters, scribed deep in the marble,
old pain and fresh agony
howling and screaming from the name:

HENRY

I speak softly,
Whisper to the winds;
The Sea answers.
She shouts in storm syllables,
Howls in hurricane stanzas,
Writes truth in tempest,
Sings of half-remembered sorrows
in shrieking gales.

You, love, with your lips sewn shut.
Me, lost in the wilderness, skin leaking poison.

The Sea spans the space between us.
The waves know you, and speak of you.
They sing of you, whisper of you.
But I don't understand all the words,
And I know I'm missing something,
Half-understood truths slipping past me,
And if only I could comprehend,
I would find you.

I smell your perfume on the wind.
I hear the soft sigh of your voice,

That dulcet sound you make
as you come apart with me.
I can almost taste your skin
in the soak of the brine on my lips.
If I stand at the prow and close my eyes,
I can almost feel you.

Darkness gathers around me;
I wear it like a cloak.
I wrap the shreds of shadows around my shoulders
like a tattered coat,
Because the light, the sun, the warmth,
They are too real, too bright, too unforgiving…
And I prefer to hide.
I am king of shadows,
wading the shoals at full moon,
storm clouds as my crown;
I play in the deeps,
cavort with the weird, translucent, eyeless creatures
which lurk there beside me.
If I emerge into the light,
you will see my ugliness.
The Sea will go glassy,
It will become a mirror,
reflecting my flaws back to me.
I don't want to see them;
I don't want you to see them.

Must I give up my crown?

Must I shed my cloak?
Must I show you all my sins,
worn on my flesh
like warts and boils and scabs?
Must I see them, myself?

You are beautiful,
You are perfect.
You are a carving of ivory,
a thing of unmarred porcelain—
flawless and elegant.
I know this is a fiction,
but such are the games played by Memory,
Such are the vagaries of Time,
Those mischievous sisters of the trickster,
The Sea.

You, love, with your lips sewn shut,
Me, lost in shadows,
skin leaking alcohol, leaking poison,
leaking truth.

You, love,
sighing in the silence.
You, love,
reaching for me with a sleepy smile.
You, love,
collapsed against a headstone, weeping.
You, love,

your spine presented to me,
You, love,
wasting away,
silence wrapped around you like ice.
You, love,
shrouded by the miles and the months.

Where are you, my love?

There's No Place Like Home: The Lighthouse At The End Of The World

A short story by
Christian St. Pierre

It is a barren, windswept island. A few scrub pines grow on it here and there, some tall, sharp-bladed grass. The entirety of the island is hilly, rising and falling, curving around and carving in, full of divots and caves and hidden folds in the granite. It looks and feels like what it is—an outcropping of rock protruding from the angry, wine-dark sea.

It is a place of importance to sailors; it marks a channel, alerting ships to the presence of nearby rocks. There is a lighthouse upon it. A residence. A barn. An acre or so of grass fenced in for a cow and her calf and a few goats. Some chickens cluck in scattered clumps around the house, and a path of uneven stone flags mark the way from the residence to the lighthouse. A small fenced-off garden grows behind the house with vegetables growing in neat rows.

The sky above is almost always clear blue, except when storms blow in, and when those storms come, they rage with all the fury of the gods.

Connor Yates is the lighthouse keeper. He is a

sullen, terse, unhappy man. Prone to bouts of heavy drinking—there was a war, and the memories of it haunt him, driving him to drink in an attempt to drown them out. It doesn't work, and he will give up the bottle for a time, only to go right back to it when the nightmares and waking moments of memory become too strong.

He has been alone on the island, tending the lighthouse, for too long—years. So long he has forgotten how to speak, he sometimes thinks. The shipping company which owns the lighthouse sends a ship twice a year, laden with supplies—haunches of dried beef, sacks of potatoes, canned fruits and vegetables, bags of corn and flour and sugar, pouches of smoking tobacco, cases of whiskey, months' and months' worth of newspapers bundled together in heavy squares and tied with twine, books, casks of ale, sides of mutton, tins of coffee and tea, bales of hay, barrels of oats and grain and seed for the animals, bullets for his rifle and pistol which he only uses for target practice as a means of passing the long boring hours, a myriad of other sundries necessary to support a man alone on an island in the middle of the ocean.

Connor is lonely, but mostly content in his solitude.

The solitude is the only balm he has found for the ragged wounds to his soul; he came away from the war unwounded in body, and this too is a source of unending guilt for him. He likes the isolation—when he wakes screaming from a nightmare, there is no one he will awaken or frighten, no one to ask him what's wrong, no one to try and wake him and perhaps be accidentally wounded, for he can become quite violent when roused from a nightmare. Which, long ago, is something Connor discovered the unhappy way, and is the reason for his self-imposed exile to this distant, desolate place: he doesn't trust himself around other people.

For all of its desolation, for all that it is far, far from anything like humanity, it is a beautiful place, wild and brutally lovely. Connor can see hundreds of miles in every direction from the tiny rim of a balcony encircling the glass of the lighthouse, which is a hundred feet tall and built upon the very highest promontory of rock on the island, another two hundred feet above sea level.

Connor finds the greatest peace—the only peace—standing on that narrow, ledge gripping the brass railing and staring out at the rippling marble field of the sea, veined with streaks of silver and jade and azure, twinkling with diamond glints on sunny days and hard and leaden on gray, stormy days. He stands facing east to watch the dawn, and returns at sundown to face west, watching the sun drown itself beneath the horizon. He is capable of standing there, forearms on the brass tube of the railing with the wind in his beard, for hours on end. The wind is always blowing, up there, hard enough to howl past his ears, hard enough to sometimes require him to grip the railing to keep from being blown off balance.

Sometimes, he thinks he could bound up onto the railing, crouch there a moment, then spread his arms like wings, leap into the sky and catch the wind and be carried away. Sometimes, he has gone so far as to grip the railing and tense his legs and prepare to leap, but then he remembers the ships, and that without him, the light would go out and the ships would crash, and more lives would be laid at his feet. More blood would coat his hands. And he then forces his hands to unclench and forces himself to relax against the rail and watch the sun, to close his eyes and feel the wind in his hair.

Time is a fickle mistress. The days and weeks and months pass unevenly. Sometimes an entire month will pass and he'll only realize it with a start, and wonder where the time went, and then he will think surely half a year has passed already, and he'll consult the calendar affixed to the wall in the kitchen, and realize only a week has passed. Time plays the same game on him with hours and minutes. Units of time are interchangeable, to Connor, in some ways.

The only way he has of marking the passage of time at all, really, is the arrival of the ship with his supplies in spring and fall, reminding him of the existence of the world beyond his little island.

The ship, in the years Connor has lived on the island tending the lighthouse, has always been captained by the same man—Elijah McKenna, a hard, swarthy man with a black beard long since gone mostly silver, skin like old leather, eyes like chips of granite, a man almost as tersely uncommunicative as Connor himself. Elijah pilots the lighter from the ship to the tiny dock himself, and helps Connor unload the supplies and then helps him haul them up to the residence. Once the work is done, the men will tamp their pipes and tipple some whiskey and sit and smoke on the porch of the residence, and Connor might remark on recent storms, and Elijah might remark on events from wider world, but on the whole, both men are content to sit and smoke and drink. They may play cards, or they may pass back and forth the pages of the most recent newspaper—many weeks and months old by this time, usually. Elijah is the only person Connor has had any contact with at all in at least three years; if there is anyone in the whole world whom Connor might call a friend, it would be Elijah.

Then, one spring, the ship arrives, and the lighter scuds up against the dock. Connor is there to accept the line and tie it off; he does so slowly, his movements listless and fumbling. His attention is not on the rope, nor the pylon to which he is tying it, but on the lighter. Instead of Elijah—stout and leathery and solid and silent, clad as always in faded dungarees and a thick wool sweater and heavy boots and an old slouch cap—there are two people; neither of them is Elijah.

One is a man on the older side of middle age, but trim and tough looking, with broad shoulders and fierce eyes, smartly dressed in a suit, with an unmistakable air of a man used to command. The other is a woman. Young. Soft. Hesitant of movement as she climbs out of the lighter onto the dock, but with confidence in her gaze, which lands on Connor and remains there, unwavering, openly curious; she is more than just pretty, or lovely; she is, truly, the most beautiful woman Connor has ever seen, and he knew many women before the war, when he was an eager young man in a sharp uniform, when the world held only possibility. She is fair of skin—her skin looks to him like cream just before it is poured into a mug of coffee. Her hair is dark, twisted into an effortlessly elegant knot behind her head. Her dress is pale green, accentuating her creamy skin and dark hair. It is not the gown of a high-born lady, but a sturdy, sensible thing, allowing her easy movement. But yet, for all that, she carries herself with an air of elegance and sophistication, which makes Connor feel uneasy and dirty and hesitant.

Once both the man and the woman—obviously his daughter, for they have the same eyes and a similar cast of feature and similar bearing—have climbed from ship's boat to the dock, Connor only stands there, staring, silent.

"Well?" the man says, his tone hard and impatient. "Best get the supplies unloaded. I'm Captain Robert Kinross, and this is my daughter, Tess. You are Connor Yates?"

Connor only grunts an affirmative, at first, then

remembers his manners in the presence of a lady. "I mean, yeah. Yes. I'm Connor." He reaches down into the lighter and hauls out a bag of potatoes, one in each hand. "Where's Elijah?"

Captain Kinross checks his pocket watch, and offers no assistance. "He took ill a few months ago. He is retired, now."

"Took ill?"

"Something to do with his heart."

"Oh." Connor stacks bags of wheat and corn. "Good man."

This is more than he's spoken all at once since the previous fall, and his voice feels rusty, the use of words an unfamiliar taste in his mouth.

The lighter is full of supplies, sagging low in the water, and even with Elijah helping it usually took the two of them half a day to unload and haul all the supplies up the island to the residence; if Captain Kinross is disinclined to help, it will take Connor the entire day and then some.

Still, he says nothing of this, only moves with slow and methodical and tireless economy, stacking all the goods on the dock and taking inventory as he does so; Captain Kinross has withdrawn a small notebook from his breast pocket and is taking notes of some kind, and Tess has found a seat on a bag of potatoes. She too has a book in hand, but hers is larger, a sketchbook, and she is busily sketching the scene. As he works, Connor takes note of her sketches—she is very good. She draws the growing stack of goods, the house up on the hill, the lighthouse high up on its perch. She draws the lighter, rocking emptily now against the dock. The ship away in the distance, sails reefed, masts and spars thin dark lines against the pale blue sky.

She even draws him. In the sketch, he is turned partially away from her with a barrel of whiskey on his shoulder and a sack of nails in his other hand. She captures in a few quick strokes the line of his jaw and the scruff of his unkempt beard, the breadth of his shoulders and the dark hollows of his deep-set eyes.

She notices his attention, and turns the book so he can see the sketch properly. "It isn't a very wonderful likeness, of course, only a hastily done sketch." She shrugs modestly. "I could do a proper portrait, if you like."

Connor only stares, unsure of a response.

"No time for that, I'm afraid," Captain Kinross says, not looking up from his writing. "We must be away soon. Time and tide wait for no man."

"But Papa, we've only just arrived," Tess says. "I should like even a short break from the ship, and besides, I want to see the lighthouse. Could Mr. Yates show me, once the supplies are in?"

"We really must be away, soon, Tess."

"Then why don't you help poor Mr. Yates with the supplies? It would be done in half the time, wouldn't it?"

Captain Kinross's eyes narrow over the top of his

notebook, and then flick from Connor to Tess and back. And then, moving slowly and reluctantly, he pockets his notebook and the stub of pencil, and begins helping Connor.

Together, the work progresses apace, and soon the supplies are stacked on the dock. Connor has been doing this long enough to have a system in place: he always unloads the items from the lighter first, and in so doing takes inventory of the incoming supplies, and compares it against the inventory of what he currently has in stock on the island—this running tally is kept in a small thick ledger wedged in his back pocket, which he hauls out and consults now and again, marking a note on this item or that, making sure nothing has been forgotten. When he is sure all the supplies brought in match his needs, he writes down on a separate sheet of paper the items he will need on the next ship in, and how much.

The first trip up the stairs from dock to residence, Tess follows the men up and makes herself at home on the porch. She takes a seat in a rocking chair and immediately opens her sketchbook and sets to work sketching the new vista—the island beneath them, the dock and the lighter, the stairs, the ship like a toy in the distance.

Several hours and many trips later, the supplies are all in and put away. Connor isn't winded at all and is barely damp with sweat, but Captain Kinross is huffing and dripping, and it is he who suggests, now the work is done, that a brief respite and refreshments would not go amiss.

And so Connor finds himself clumsily attempting to make sandwiches and coffee. He has made rather a mess of the sandwiches and the coffee has been percolating and bubbling, and it is just then, as he is beginning to feel flustered and overwhelmed at the unfamiliar task of preparing food for more than merely himself, that Tess appears in the doorway.

"Your coffee is burning, I believe," she remarks.

Connor just grunts—an alternative to the curse he wishes to let loose—and snags the coffee off the top of the wood-burning stove. He burns his fingers, only just managing to not drop the pot, but in so doing knocks the sandwiches to the floor.

Shaking his hand, he snarls a curse, and then blushes with a glance at Tess. "Apologies, ma'am."

Tess only laughs. "Don't be silly. I live onboard a ship, surrounded by sailors. There's nothing you could say that would shock me." She surveys the mess he's made. "Would you like some help, Mr. Yates?"

"Ain't no mister. Just call me Connor," he grumbles. "Guests aren't supposed to see to their own refreshments."

Tess laughs again. "Yes, well, I don't mind." She makes quick work of sweeping and binning the mess on the floor, and then sets to remaking the sandwiches. "I am hungry, and this is work I'm rather more suited to than you, it would seem."

Connor watches as she accomplishes in moments what it took him minutes to do. "Don't get people round here often," he says by way of explanation.

"Twice a year, as Father explains it. From what I understand, you've only had Captain Elijah to visit twice a year for the last several years."

Connor manages a noise of affirmation.

"Don't you get lonely?" Tess asks.

He lifts a shoulder. "Some."

She arranges the sandwiches onto a plate, but doesn't move to carry them out to the porch yet. "I should think I would be dreadfully lonely here, all by myself for months on end."

"Used to it," he murmurs, rinsing out coffee mugs so long unused that they're dirty with dust. "Ain't really much for company anyhow."

She looks at him with an odd light in her eyes. "I don't think I'd mind it here at all, so long as I had one other person to talk to."

He catches something in her voice, some potential for hidden meaning. "Ain't no place for a lady, Miss Kinross. This place barely counts as livable, except for a solitary fella like myself."

"I think I'm rather capable of determining for myself what is and is not livable to me." She smiles at him. "Most would say a ship full of coarse men out on the open sea for months at a time is also no place for a lady, yet such is where I have lived the last ten years of my life."

"Ain't got no kin? Nowhere more decent to live?"

She frowns. "I've a very distant aunt or cousin or some such, living in Suffolk, or somewhere like that. I'd rather be with Papa. I like the sea, and I like the open places. I feel confined and constricted when we visit cities."

He wonders about her mother, but doesn't dare ask. "Last time I was in a city, I damn near stopped breathing 'til I got clear of it. Too many folks and not enough air." He winces, and rubs the back of his neck. "I shouldn't curse. Hard habit to break."

This is more than he's said all at once since the end of the war.

The strange conversation ends then, when Captain Kinross calls out a query regarding refreshments. By the time the coffee has been drunk and the sandwiches eaten, it is dark. Elijah never cared much about having to row back to the ship in the dark, but Captain Kinross is a different sort of man entirely, and to expect a woman to make such a trip is unthinkable. There is one extra bedroom, which Tess takes, and Captain Kinross takes Connor's bed; Connor tries unsuccessfully to sleep on a chair in the sitting room. He knew the moment he closed his eyes that he would suffer from the dreams again, and with company in the house didn't dare risk waking them up with his screams; he abandons all pretense of sleep. Instead, he puts on a pot of coffee, pours himself a mug, and carries it with him up to the lighthouse.

He settles into his usual place, leaning against the railing, watching the moon arc across the sky.

He hears a noise behind him, but dismisses it as the settling of the building, so unused is he to company. Thus, when a hand alights on his shoulders, he is badly startled, cursing viciously as he whirls and steps away, spilling coffee as he draws a knife from a sheath on his belt, his teeth bared.

Tess, candle in one hand, backs away, frightened. "I'm—I'm sorry, I—I didn't mean to startle you."

Embarrassed, he turns away. "I'm the one to apologize, Miss Kinross. Told you, I ain't much used to havin' folks around."

She tiptoes cautiously onto the balcony, moving slowly, clinging to the railing with her free hand, peering over the edge nervously. "We're very high up."

"Some four hundred feet above the sea, where we're standing. Thereabouts, leastways. Less directly to the ground, though."

"Don't you get frightened? The wind is so strong. I'm afraid it'll just pluck me up and carry me away."

Indeed, the wind is very strong. It whips her hair behind her in a straight black line, and plasters her nightdress against her body. Connor notices this, tries not to stare and is only partially successful.

"Sometimes, I think I could just fly away," Connor hears himself say. "Just…let the wind take me wherever it is the wind goes."

"If I wasn't so scared of falling, I'd think that was

a lovely sentiment indeed." A rough gust of flattering wind pushes at them, and Tess shrieks and shrinks against Connor's side. "Oh, how frightening!"

Connor lets her weight lean against him, keeping a strong grip on the railing with one hand, nursing his coffee in the other. "Forget I said that. The wind ain't gonna hurt you none. Just hold on tight and you'll be fine."

She holds on tight, all right, but to him rather than the railing. "I'd rather you held me, Connor." The words are daring, put out there in the open like that, so boldly.

"You don't know a durn thing about me, Miss Kinross. I ain't fit company for a lady like yourself."

"I'm the daughter of a sailor—I'm no lady. I've spent more time on the deck of a ship than among proper society, and I can read the sea more easily than I can the newspaper." She pulls away, then, straightening her spine and turning to face the sea. "I know myself, Mr. Yates. I know what I want."

"You've been here not even a day. Come winter, the storms have real teeth. And there wouldn't be anyone around, not anyone at all 'cept me. Not for months and months at a time. No way to change your mind once you see how things is."

"I've weathered hurricanes and typhoons, helped fight off brigands, seen men hung, keelhauled, and thrown overboard. We've been becalmed several times, nearly sunk twice, and I once ordered a man flogged for rape when my father was ashore conducting business."

She turns to face Connor, then. "I know myself, Mr. Yates."

Connor has no idea how to respond to this, and so he doesn't. Silence breathes between them, and Tess seems content to let the silence be, rather than needing to fill it with chatter, as he'd have expected.

After a while, she turns to Connor again. "Will you walk me back down?"

"O'course."

The walk down the stairs is long, and she seems to push ever closer against his side as they descend, and her hand continually brushes against his. This, for some reason, makes his heart pound worse than the first battle he fought, in the moments before his line rushed the enemy.

Tess pauses at the bottom of the stair, plucking at Connor's sleeve. "Wait a moment, please."

He stops, turns back to face her, the door behind him. "Yes, Miss Kinross?"

She stares up at him. "Call me Tess."

"All right."

"I like you, Connor."

He just blinks at her. "Not rightly sure why, ma'am." He rubs the back of his neck. "I ain't good company."

"You seem like perfectly agreeable company to me."

"The war, you see. It...did things to me, here and here." He taps his temple, and then his heart. "You saw what happened when you startled me."

"Not all of the men on my father's boat are chosen

for their skill as sailors, Connor." There's a subtext to her words, which Connor reads easily. "I'm not afraid of you."

"We just met, Tess."

"I know. But I know myself. And I know what I want."

"What is it you want, then?"

"A quiet life, away from the crowds and the cities. A home near the sea. Solitude, and a good man to keep me company. A child, perhaps, someday."

Connor's collar suddenly feels too tight, and his chest wouldn't expand all the way. "I—Tess, I—"

She just smiles at him. "Think about it, perhaps?" Her hair drifts across her face, hiding a smirk and a burst of soft laughter. "You'll have several months in which to consider the idea, after all."

She's passed him, then, out the door and tiptoeing across the stone flags, her candle guttering in the wind. He watches her lithe, lush form, an uneasy, unfamiliar rush of something sharp and hot and tense filling him at the sight of her body, highlighted by the way the wind blows her nightdress against her curves. She stops at the back door, and the wind shifts, pushing the nightdress against her breasts and between her thighs, and his mouth goes dry and he feels dizzy and the sharp hot tense feeling intensifies, until he recognizes it as desire and lust and something deeper, something more.

He has a small cot up at the top of the lighthouse,

in case a storm blows up and he has to doze by the light, to keep it lit the night through. Here, Connor sleeps, fitfully. He dreams odd dreams, full of desires he thought he'd forgotten long ago, in his quest for solitude.

Next morning, she is awake before he is and bustling about the kitchen, preparing a more hearty breakfast than any he'd had even before he joined the army. She smiles at him at odd moments, brightening a face already so beautiful it makes Connor's heart ache.

Her father notices, Connor is certain.

When it is time for Captain Kinross and his daughter to return to the ship, Connor walks them down. Captain Kinross goes ahead a few steps, and Tess walks in stride with Connor.

"I had hoped you would take my hand yesterday night, as we descended the stair," she murmurs to him, as they walk together. "Or that you would have kissed me, there at the landing."

"I don't know if I could be so bold," Connor says. "You're so beautiful, I'd think I was…taking airs above my station, or somethin' of the like."

"Don't be ridiculous," Tess says. "I don't think THAT for stations, or airs, or any of that nonsense." On the emphasized word, she snaps her fingers. "But I do thank you for your compliment."

Connor walks a few paces more in silence, considering his words carefully, as he always does. "I'm not a clever man, nor an ambitious one, Tess. This is what

I've chosen for my lot in life. I don't know that I'd be good company for a woman, nor a child. If you're having me on, then leave off the game. And if you're serious, then you as well have many months to consider if this is really the life you'd like."

She seems to drag words out of him, great floods of words he didn't know he possessed.

Tess just smiles at him, and presses something into his palm, discreetly. "I am not a woman to play games, Connor, be assured of that. And furthermore, I neither need nor want cleverness nor ambition in a man. Only truth, protection, and love. And, perhaps...passion." Here, she gazes up at him, and her eyes are full of innuendo he doesn't miss, which makes his heart pound and his chest feel constricted. "Do you think you could possess those qualities, Mr. Yates?"

"I think—I think I could learn, if a body was patient in the teaching."

They are interrupted, then, by a call from Captain Kinross. "Tess, darling. We must go." To Connor, then. "Mr. Yates. A word."

The men pace away from the dock, out of earshot of Tess, who sits in the lighter. "This is no place for a woman, Mr. Yates, and certainly not my daughter. Nothing said against you, mind, but—"

"I've expressed much the same to Tess myself, Captain. You've a headstrong daughter on your hands, sir."

Captain Kinross laughs good-naturedly. "Indeed I

do, Mr. Yates. Indeed I do." He claps the younger man on the shoulder. "Well, we'll be off, now. And if she's still interested when we come back for our fall visit, well…I'm not sure I could stop her if I wanted to, and by all accounts, you're a good man."

"She's a rarely fine woman, Captain. I wouldn't ask her to choose this life…but if she did? Well, sir, I'd consider it a greater honor than a man like me deserves."

Connor watches the ship depart, standing at the rail of his lighthouse. He can't see nearly so far, but his imagination provides for him a vision of Tess, standing at the stern, wind tossing her hair sideways and her dress against her thigh; perhaps, to her, he is a speck near the top of the white spire. He wonders if she will be back.

He hopes, for his sake, that she will be; and for hers, that she won't.

As she'd said, Connor has all the months of spring and summer to wonder. He thinks of the moments spent with her at the top of the lighthouse, and the descent down the stairs, her hand brushing his, and the words they exchanged at the landing. He thinks of the things she'd said on the way down to the dock, that last day, and the way she'd looked up at him. As if a creature so lovely and elegant and wonderful and angelic could look at a man like him and see him with anything like the desire he feels for her.

As such things go, he plays in his mind the few moments they'd shared together over and over again, until each individual second with her is imprinted on his mind like a tintype image. He imagines the things she might say if she returns, and what he would say. Sometimes he chastises himself as a fool, wasting his time on romantic notions which could never see fruition, and sometimes he thinks perhaps she might arrive on the next ship, and he would be there on the dock waiting as the lighter drifted slowly from ship to shore, and she would alight from the vessel and she would be in his arms, and her eyes, so like the color of the Caribbean sea at high bright noon, would fix on his and neither would have to say anything—they would just know.

Time, ever the miscreant, ever the mischievous mistress, plays its usual tricks upon Connor, dragging days out to feel like weeks, and weeks like months, then compacting months into the space of a week, and he finds himself watching the eastern sea for signs of the ship. He finds himself consulting his calendar and marking days off, when he used to barely care for the arrival of the ship at all, except that it meant fresh food and new spirits and the occasional batch of news from beyond his island, and perhaps the silent company of Elijah.

Now, though, he finds himself waiting for the ship with impatience he'd never known before. It bothers him, his impatience. His hope. That hope frightens him—to survive alone in so desolate a place requires a certain numbness, an apathy, a willful lack of concern for the company of others, disdain for what the future might hold.

Until Tess, each day of Connor's future held the same as the day before; now, though, the future holds something else: the unknown. Possibility.

It is a tantalizing thing.

He still spends much of his time at the railing of the lighthouse, watching the sun rise and set. In his hands, he holds the small square of paper she'd handed him upon her departure, now wrinkled and thin from much folding and unfolding. The wind plucks it, trying to snatch it away, but he holds it firmly. On the paper are written a few words in a neat, looping, feminine script:

I SHALL BE A VERY PATIENT TEACHER, MR. YATES.
—TESS

He reads this over and over again, thinking back to that conversation, and hoping that her note means she will return, and that she will want him.

Folded into the square of paper had been a scrap of lace, which smelled of perfume, of woman. He isn't at all sure where the lace had come from, and his imagination plays tantalizing tricks on him, suggesting all kinds of possibilities. It really is just a scrap of lace, a few small inches of fabric that could have come from a handkerchief or a bedspread or the rags of an old dress. But it smells of her, the way he remembered her smelling.

He keeps this piece of lace folded into a scrap of cloth and tucked away in his Bible, a generations-old keepsake handed down from grandfather to grandson. The note he keeps in his pocket, and withdraws to read often.

And so, he waits.

He lives the life he's always lived, there on the remote island, going about his daily chores the way he always has; nothing has changed. But yet…all is changed. She changed things just by existing, by offering even the faintest ray of hope.

No, he tells himself. Don't be absurd. You are a silent, sullen, soldier prone to nightmares, he tells himself. You drink too much. You live on a remote island far from civilization. You have nothing to offer anyone, let alone a vibrant, funny, beautiful woman like Tess Kinross—

She said it herself, though, he argues back: she knows what she wants. And she made rather clear what she wanted—

Unless you were imagining that—

The note referring to our conversation doesn't leave much room for misunderstanding, though—

And so, around and around it goes.

Days, weeks, and months more, stretching and compacting. The air grows cooler and he harvests his vegetables—he knows from the inventory tally in his ledger that the ship is due soon.

He is in his garden, turning over the soil so it will go fallow for the following spring. His back aches, and his hands are blistered from the rough handle of the hoe. He straightens, stretching his lower back, resting the hoe against his shoulder and rubbing his stinging palms on his trousers.

There, off in the distance, is the ship. Anchored, sails furled. He can almost make out the bustle of activity on the deck, tiny specks hustling to and fro, the shadowy outline of the lighter as it is lowered.

His heart pounds.

Is she on that lighter?

Will eight months of the wide, complex, interesting world beyond this isolated shore have changed her mind?

He turns back to his work, knowing it will be quite some time before the lighter is loaded and longer yet before it can make the trip from ship to shore. He finishes turning over the garden, washes his hands at the well pump, goes inside to change his shirt. Pausing at the mirror by the front door, he examines his reflection—his wild, long, tangled hair, his unkempt beard.

He stumbles hurriedly to the bedroom, finds a comb on the bureau, drags it through his hair and his beard. His reflection, then, is somewhat more presentable—but his shirt is buttoned wrong.

He curses his foolishness, and takes a deep breath. Considers stopping in the kitchen for a slug of whiskey to fortify his nerves, but rejects the idea—Tess would not want to shackle herself to a drunkard.

He is a mass of jangling nerves by the time the lighter arrives, and his heart sinks when only Captain Kinross is in the boat. Tying off the line, Connor begins immediately retrieving supplies, without a word. Captain Kinross helps him, handing up bags and sacks and barrels and crates. Not a word is spoken until the lot is piled on the dock and tallied, and then Kinross ascends to the dock, wipes his forehead with a kerchief, and settles his weight on the top of a barrel.

"You were hoping to see Tess, unless I'm mistaken," Kinross says.

Connor just nods.

"She took ill in the weeks before we departed." Captain Kinross delves a hand in the breast pocket of his suit coat. "A dreadful case of influenza. She would have taken berth for this journey even ill, but I feared for her life, and forbade it."

"She will recover, then?" Connor asks.

"Oh, most certainly. Her anger at me may not, but her health will." Kinross hands Connor an envelope. "She bade me give you this."

"I see." Connor takes the letter, slices it open with his knife then and there, and withdraws the letter.

MY DEAREST CONNOR,

CURSE THIS ILLNESS, AND MY BODY FOR SUCCUMBING! I HAVE MISSED YOU MUCH THESE PAST MONTHS. I

HAVE SPENT NEARLY EVERY WAKING MOMENT THINKING OF YOU, AND I LOOK FORWARD MOST EAGERLY TO OUR REUNION. I DO NOT DARE LEAVE SUCH WEIGHTY MATTERS AS OUR FUTURE TO THE VAGARIES OF TIME AND THE CAPRICE OF THE SEA, AND SO I RISK ALL WITH AS MUCH FORWARDNESS AS I POSSESS:

IF YOU SHALL HAVE ME, I WOULD BE YOUR WIFE.

I KNOW WELL THIS IS NOT HOW SUCH MATTERS ARE CUSTOMARILY ARRANGED, BUT I AM FAR TOO IMPATIENT TO WAIT. IF YOU DESIRE THIS UNION, ASK MY FATHER FOR MY HAND WHILE HE IS THERE, AND TELL HIM I HAVE ALREADY AGREED. THEN, I WILL, WHETHER SICK OR HALE, JOIN YOU ON YOUR—NAY, ON OUR ISLAND—AS YOUR WIFE. IF YOU SHOULD AGREE, I WILL BE MRS. CONNOR YATES BY THE COMING SPRING.

WITH ALL OF MY LOVE, AND MORE YET TO COME,

SOON TO BE YOURS,

TESS

Connor reads the letter through a dozen times before the meaning and the import of the contents truly sink into his head and his heart.

"Well?" Captain Kinross grumbles. "What does she say?"

Connor blows out a breath, considering his next words with great care. "She regrets her absence, and curses her illness."

"Is that all?" Kinross's voice betrays doubt, and not a little amusement. "I seem to see more words upon the page than that."

Connor nods, reading it through yet again. "She bids me—" He stops, teeth clicking down on his words. "What I mean to say, sir, is that I humbly beg you for your daughter's hand in marriage."

Kinross is quiet a moment, considering. "Well, I do admit this is not momentously shocking news to me. You were, these past months, nearly all my daughter would speak of."

"Sir, I—"

Kinross interrupts. "Connor—Mr. Yates. Answer me this: is this marriage your idea, or hers?"

Connor just blinks. "Both."

"You told me, last we spoke, that I have a headstrong daughter on my hands. You little know how much so, I fear. I would not want to see her suffer for getting what she thinks she wants, and coming to regret it. Your isolation here is total, for the majority of the year."

Connor nods. "I said so to her myself, back in the spring. I believe I love her, sir, and will love her all the more every day, if I should be so honored as to have her as my wife. I would never begrudge her the chance to change her mind. If she were to ever want to leave, if she grew to hate this place, I would see her gone on the next ship, so she could find her happiness elsewhere. But yet, as long as she willfully desires to be my wife, I will love her and protect her with all that I am." He is nearly panting with exertion, having used so many words all at once, and so properly.

Captain Kinross nods. "I believe you. You have my blessing."

The rest of the visit passes swiftly—without Tess, the men find little to speak of, and so waste little time transferring the various goods to the residence and packing them away. There is a pot of coffee, a little food, less conversation, and then Captain Kinross makes his departure.

Standing on his lighthouse, Connor watches the ship vanish over the horizon. He finds it little coincidence that the ship vanishes from sight at the exact moment of sundown, when the last orange slice of sun sinks under the horizon, and he takes it as a portent of good fortune when the rim of the bright yellow-orange-crimson orb flashes green.

Another moment, and the sun is gone.

Now comes the long, cruel winter. Storms, and bitter cold. Endless wind, sharper than razors. Deep nights, dull days.

It is, in every way possible, the longest and most lonely winter Connor has ever known.

Eagerness to see Tess consumes him, and stretches the passing of the weeks and months out to unbearable agony. It is worsened by the fact that there could be no letters in the meantime, even if could he find the words to put on paper. He tries, just for practice, but his penmanship is so awful and the few words he did manage so clumsy that he burns the scraps of paper.

The waiting is torture, and with the storms raging so frequently and the cold so brutal, there is little enough for him to do besides sit in the lighthouse and tend the light. He very nearly lives up there, that winter. He has a stockpile of bits of wood of odd shapes and sizes, and he whiles away the time whittling, carving little figures, likenesses of horses and wolves and bison and whales and dogs and roosters, until he has enough to fill a crate.

The storms fade, flowers bloom, and warmth returns.

His inventory tells him the ship is due soon—he's nearly out of coffee, sugar, tobacco, and wheat, which he very carefully rations.

Then, on a sunny but cool evening, he spies the ship cresting the horizon, spurring a freshet of panic in him.

He quells it, with difficulty.

As the lighter approaches, he combs his hair and beard, changes into fresh clothing; he considers attempting to trim his hair and beard, but decides against it—she claimed a desire to marry him as he is, so why attempt to change himself into something else? If she wants his hair and beard trimmed, perhaps she will do it herself.

He does, however, find himself waiting on the dock, impatiently whittling away at a block of wood, slowly revealing the shape of a flower.

He finishes the flower when the lighter is still only halfway between ship and shore, and so he pulls out a scrap of sandpaper out of his pocket and sets to work smoothing out the edges. He has little enough to offer Tess, and this, at least, is something of his own doing which he can present as a token of his affection.

At long last, the lighter comes to rest against the dock. Within the lighter, aside from the supplies, are Captain Kinross, Tess, a black-clad priest or minister—Connor is not a religious man, and little knows the difference—and a handful of men who must be ship's crew—the first mate, the bosun, and the quartermaster, most likely.

Connor's nerves thrum into life, then, at the sight of so many people. He has not encountered so many people all at once since the war, and he finds his heart squeezing and clotting in his throat, his pulse hammering wildly, irrational fears racing in his mind.

Then his eyes land on Tess, and all quiets within him.

She is wearing a yellow dress, and it is not designed for practicality this time, but for allure. The neck is scooped almost indecently low, and it hugs her waist and hips, and when she steps from lighter to dock, Connor sees a glimpse of her calf. Her eyes dance merrily, happily, as she drifts across the dock to where Connor stands, one hand in his trouser pocket, the other clutching the carven flower.

Tess stops mere inches from him, gazing up. "Why Connor, you've combed your hair and beard."

"Probably needs a bit of a trim," he mumbles.

She only smiles. "Nonsense." She reaches up and runs her fingers through his beard. "You're quite handsome just like this."

"Your dress is…" he hems and haws, and tries again. "You're the loveliest woman I ever saw."

"Thank you, Connor. I purchased it especially for this day."

He just stares down at Tess, drinking in her face, the black luster of her hair, the vivid azure of her eyes, the pale cream of her skin. "You're here. Felt like you'd never get here, some days."

Her hand rests on his chest. "Oh, the voyage here was absolutely interminable! And Papa even says we made excellent time. I just…I couldn't bear a single minute apart from you."

"Thought I'd dreamed it all."

"So did I."

"You…you really want to be here? With me?"

"There's nowhere I'd rather be, and no one I'd rather be with, than here, with you."

"Why?" He can't help the question. "Why me?"

She combs her fingers through his beard again, her touch gentle and affectionate. "My heart chose you. The moment I stepped onto this dock and saw you, I knew. And when I stepped off the dock the last time, I knew I'd be back. And now that I've returned, I just know..."

"Know what?"

"I shan't be leaving again. I'm home, now."

"I'm not much for pretty talk, Tess." He steps a little closer, so he can almost feel her body against his, a tease, a ghost of a touch, a promise. "But if you're patient, and you're willing, I'll learn how to love you. That's about the best I can promise."

"I don't care overly much for fancy words. I can get those in books, if that's what I want." She takes his hands in hers. "I just want you, Connor. Just as you are. Gruff, and quiet, and dependable."

"Don't deserve you, Tess."

"That's the thing about love, Connor—it's not something we earn, or deserve. We have only to accept it, and give all we have in return."

He hesitates a moment, and then shows her the flower he carved for her. She takes the carving and examines it with surprise and joy.

"Why, Connor! I had no idea you were such an artisan!" She tucks it into the valley of her bosom, and then returns her gaze to Connor's.

"It's just...I just wanted to have something to give you."

"It's lovely. I shall treasure it always."

Behind Tess, the other men were unloading the goods, but for once, Connor let himself stay still, let himself just stand and hold the woman who had decided she was his, and he hers.

"I got one question, though," he murmurs.

She smiles softly up at him. "Which is what?"

"The lace, that bit of lace you gave me with the note." He hesitates, and then continues. "Where's it from? What'd you cut it out of?"

Her smile is less soft, and more playful. "Well, Connor, I'm not sure it's proper or decent that I tell you." She tugs on his beard, an eyebrow quirked up. "You'll have to wait until after we're married to find that out."

His face heats. "Oh. The wondering has been eating at me, these months."

"You won't have to wonder long." She glances at the minister, who has remained in the boat, perusing a passage in his Bible. "Reverend Galloway can marry us today."

"Today?"

She nods, and then eyes him quizzically. "Unless you've a reason to want to wait?"

"No!" he protests, a little too suddenly. "No." He eyes the cluster of men standing around the pile of supplies. "There's no one else you want with you for the wedding?"

"My mother died many years ago, and I've spent

most of my life aboard ship with these men. They're nearly as much my family as Papa." She pats his chest. "And really, all I need is you."

"You have me." He gestures at the island. "This place…it's all I have to offer, Tess."

"As long as you're here, I shall be more than happy."

He shakes his head, not quite able to dislodge the lingering doubt and disbelief. "You're sure, Tess? I know I've asked this more than once, I just…I need you to be sure. About me, and about this life."

She laughs, then. "I've had a year to think on this, Connor—a year to consider the hardships, the realities, and the dangers. I've thought of little else, all this time." Her hand comes to rest on his cheek. "I am absolutely sure this is what I want. I have not a single doubt. Not one." A glance at her father, and the other men, huddled together, trying to light their pipes despite the wind. "Now. Kiss me, quickly, while they're distracted."

Her lips are softer than velvet, and warm, and damp, and she tastes of something sweet. It is a moment only, a promise of a kiss, lips on lips for mere seconds, but Time plays its trick on Connor, and he feels the kiss to last a lifetime, and more.

They are married just outside the garden, with the sun setting. Tess clutches a spray of daisies and gardenias Connor has grown, and she wears a white dress, which leaves Connor's breath coming short and pulse hammering hard, and he wears his only suit. There is a time of conviviality afterward with the captain and the other officers, a bottle of wine brought by Captain Kinross for the occasion is opened and shared, and then, with a few tears on the part of Tess, and a gruff, huffing hug by the captain, the lighter departs. Connor and Tess watch it shrink across the water, watch it be drawn up into the ship, and then the ship's sails drop down and belly out in the stiff wind. A cannon blasts once, a farewell, and then the ship slowly dwindles over the horizon.

"Well, husband?" Tess, finally, turns and rests her hands on Connor's chest, and her eyes betray a myriad of heated emotions Connor has trouble believing are real, and meant for him. "We are alone, now."

"So we are."

"I bet if you explored a bit, you might find out where I cut that bit of lace from." She brushes a lock of his hair away. "You'd have to make rather bold in your exploration, however."

"Should we…" he glances up at the house, "should we go up, first?"

Tess lifts a shoulder in answer. "We could. But it is a beautiful and warm evening, and your coat upon the dock would make a fine cushion, and there is, after all, no one around to see us."

"Here?" He is surprised.

"Anywhere, Connor. Everywhere."

"Will I ever cease to be surprised by you?"

She unbuttons the top of his shirt. "I most certainly hope not, my husband."

His fingers are clumsy, seeking the buttons of her dress, at her back, but she is patient, and allows him to fumble.

She is patient, indeed, as he spends long moments freeing her from her many layers, and eventually, she is clad in only bits of silk and lace, there on the dock, and he discovers that she'd cut the lace from the inside of her most intimate unmentionable, where the lace lay against her skin.

He gazes at her for long moments.

She reaches for his clothing, and removes it item by item, until he is clad as she—that is to say, nearly not at all. And then she smiles up at him. "There is clothing yet to remove, Connor," she says. "I've dreamed of this moment with you more than I dare admit."

"I didn't dare dream of this at all."

"Then touch me, my love, and find out that this is not a dream."

"You'll always be my dream, Tess."

"And you said you weren't one for pretty words." She breathes a laugh of delight as he finally, finally, runs a hesitant, questing hand over her skin.

Later, lying tangled together on the dock, she gazes at him, happy, replete, and full of joy. "I don't think passion is something I'll need to teach you, Connor. You seem to have quite a firm grasp of that all on your own."

He laughs with her, and shows her again all the things he feels for her, which he doesn't have the words for.

He doesn't need words, he discovers. She is eager and willing to learn in other ways, and shows him her own love, thus.

In the years that follow, the dreams loosen their grip on him. When a nightmare does rack him, Tess never wakes him, only clings to him when he does awaken, screaming, and she is quick to soothe him with kisses and words of comfort and love, and soon even the dreams are as distant a memory as the war itself.

With Tess at his side, the island becomes truly home, somewhere to LIVE, not just subsist.

Also by

J Wilder

Visit me at my website: **www.jasindawilder.com**
Email me: **jasindawilder@gmail.com**

If you enjoyed this book, you can help others enjoy it as well by recommending it to friends and family, or by mentioning it in reading and discussion groups and online forums. You can also review it on the site from which you purchased it. But, whether you recommend it to anyone else or not, thank you *so much* for taking the time to read my book! Your support means the world to me!

My other titles:

Preacher's Son:
Unbound
Unleashed
Unbroken

Delilah's Diary:
A Sexy Journey
La Vita Sexy
A Sexy Surrender

Big Girls Do It:
Boxed Set
Married
On Christmas
Pregnant

Rock Stars Do It:
Harder
Dirty
Forever

From the world of *Big Girls* and *Rock Stars*:
Big Love Abroad

Biker Billionaire:
Wild Ride

The Falling Series:
Falling Into You
Falling Into Us
Falling Under
Falling Away
Falling For Colton

The Ever Trilogy:
Forever & Always
After Forever
Saving Forever

The world of *Wounded:*
Wounded
Captured

The world of *Stripped:*
Stripped
Trashed

The world of *Alpha:*
Alpha
Beta
Omega
Harris: Alpha One Security Book 1
Thresh: Alpha One Security Book 2
Duke Alpha One Security Book 3
Puck: Alpha One Security Book 4
Lear: Alpha One Security Book 5
Anselm: Alpha One Security Book 6

The Houri Legends:
Jack and Djinn
Djinn and Tonic

The Madame X Series:
Madame X
Exposed
Exiled

The Black Room
(With Jade London):
Door One
Door Two
Door Three
Door Four
Door Five
Door Six
Door Seven
Door Eight

The One Series
The Long Way Home
Where the Heart Is
There's No Place Like Home

Badd Brothers:
*Badd Motherf*cker*
Badd Ass
Badd to the Bone
Good Girl Gone Badd
Badd Luck
Badd Mojo
Big Badd Wolf
Badd Boy
Badd Kitty
Badd Business
Badd Medicine
Badd Daddy

Dad Bod Contracting:
Hammered
Drilled
Nailed
Screwed

Fifty States of Love:
Pregnant in Pennsylvania
Cowboy in Colorado
Married in Michigan

Standalone titles:
Yours

Non-Fiction titles:
You Can Do It
You Can Do It: Strength
You Can Do It: Fasting

Jack Wilder Titles:
The Missionary

JJ Wilder Titles:
Ark

To be informed of new releases, special offers, and other Jasinda news, sign up for Jasinda's email newsletter.

www.ingramcontent.com/pod-product-compliance
Lightning Source LLC
Chambersburg PA
CBHW031124090426
42738CB00008B/967

* 9 7 8 1 9 4 8 4 4 5 3 9 9 *